Meet the demands of your life with energy that goes
beyond vitamins, aerobics and positive thinking!

# SUPERNATURAL

# ENERGY

## FOR YOUR

# DAILY RACE

**A Five-Minute a Day Program
to Help You Tap into God's Power
for Everyday Living**

# Charles Mylander

## Regal Books

A Division of GL Publications
Ventura, California, U.S.A.

Published by Regal Books
A Division of GL Publications
Ventura, California 93006
Printed in U.S.A.

**Library of Congress Cataloging-in-Publication Data**

Mylander, Charles.
    Supernatural energy for the struggle : daily action for busy people / Chuck
Mylander.
        p.    cm.
    Includes bibliographical references.
    ISBN 0-8307-1363-8
    1. Christian life. 2. Power (Christian theology) I. Title.
BV4501.2.M95      1989
248.4—dc20                                                                89-38109
                                                                              CIP

**1 2 3 4 5 6 7 8 9 10 / CG KP / 92 91 90**

Rights for publishing this book in other languages are contracted by Gospel
Literature International (GLINT) foundation. GLINT also provides technical
help for the adaptation, translation, and publishing of Bible study resources
and books in scores of languages worldwide. For further information, contact
GLINT, Post Office Box 488, Rosemead, California, 91770, U.S.A., or the
publisher.

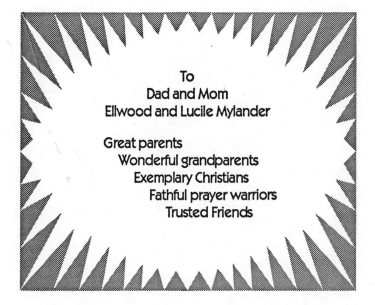

To
Dad and Mom
Ellwood and Lucile Mylander

Great parents
Wonderful grandparents
Exemplary Christians
Fathful prayer warriors
Trusted Friends

# Contents

# Acknowledgments

My heart fills with praise to God for the people who have helped make this book a reality. My gratitude goes to:

Readers of the weekly publication, *The Encourager*, in which many of the segments in this book first appeared. Their warm response encouraged me.

The staff of the Friends Church Southwest Headquarters where I work. Their enthusiastic support is heartening.

Karen Standen, who spent multiplied hours inputting this material into the word processor and bringing it out in first-rate manuscript form. Her keen interest in every detail lifted my spirits (and the editor's).

Earl Roe, the competent Regal Books editor, whose professional touch and wise counsel were invaluable. His praise was energizing.

The Gospel Light/Regal Books staff who work with such genuine appreciation for their authors. Their determination to do their best for their Lord is noteworthy.

My family—wife Nancy, son Kirk and daughter Lisa—who kept me in balance (and at times teased me off-balance). Their love is special.

The Lord Jesus Himself who gives the supernatural energy so abundantly promised in His Word. He is unspeakably wonderful.

Yorba Linda, California
June 1989

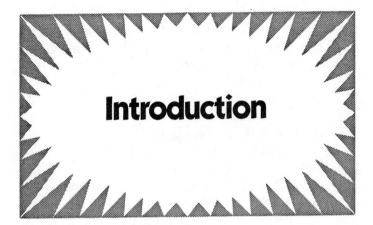

# Introduction

## Sunday/Winning the Struggle

This book is for busy people. And it is an action book, not a devotional book.

Knowing you are busy, I timed some of the daily segments. When I read them aloud they took only two to five minutes each. I expect that you will read much faster silently. In just three months of reading one segment per day you will finish the book—with thirteen weeks to practice the insights. For groups, each Sunday is devoted to discussion questions on the previous week.

Most people understand physical energy and motivational energy. A strong body and an inspired mind do indeed keep us going.

But another totally different kind of energy is also available—supernatural energy. The Bible teaches it and committed Christians experience it.

Supernatural energy goes beyond mere human strength and mental resources. It taps into the power of God. It gives stability, insight, inspiration, rejuvenation, renewal, vim, vigor and vitality.

> Do you not know?
> Have you not heard?
> The Lord is the everlasting God,
> the Creator of the ends of the earth.
> He will not grow tired or weary,
> and his understanding no one can fathom.
> He gives strength to the weary
> and increases the power of the weak.
> Even youths grow tired and weary,
> and young men stumble and fall;
> but those who hope in the Lord
> will renew their strength.
> They will soar on wings like eagles;
> they will run and not grow weary,
> they will walk and not be faint.
>
> (Isa. 40:28-31)

This book is also for people who struggle.

> Most everyone struggles—
> over finances,
> on the job,
> with family conflicts,
> in serving Christ and others.
> Jesus struggled.
> Think of His spending whole nights in prayer,
> coping with personnel problems among The Twelve,

sweating blood in Gethsemane,
    dying on a cross in agony.
Paul struggled.
    His New Testament epistles reflect an inner toil,
    an all-out combat. He struggled in
        outright suffering,
            hard work,
                personal caring and
                    concern for the churches.

I struggle and you struggle—at least at times.
What turns struggle into winning is *supernatural energy.*
It's available.
    Meditate on these verses from the Bible.

> *"I labor, struggling with all [Christ's] energy, which
> so powerfully works in me" (Col. 1:29).*
> *"It is God who [supernaturally energizes you] works
> in you to will and to act according to his good
> purpose" (Phil. 2:13).*

*Supernatural energy for the struggle can be yours!*

---

Pray for supernatural energy.
Work on applying it to your greatest struggle.

---

### Introductory Discussion Questions

1. Brainstorm a list of the most common struggles Christians face today.

2. Place a check by the items on this list where supernatural energy would help.
3. What is your greatest struggle?
4. Do you ever feel the need for more energy? Supernatural energy?
5. In your opinion, does Christ give us a "totally different kind of energy" that differs from physical or mental energy? Is supernatural energy a different sort of power or simply an increase of natural human energy?
6. Describe a time when you experienced supernatural energy beyond what you expected. What did it feel like? How did it help you? Why do you think God provided it?
7. Why do you think some Christians have so much energy for the Lord while others wear out so soon?

# ONE
# SUPERNATURAL ENERGY

Sometimes God's power comes in flashes of glory and sometimes it comes in quiet excitement. Sometimes we see Him work in spectacular miracles and sometimes in bringing unity out of division.

At the Ecumenical Missionary Conference held in New York in April 1900, Hudson Taylor spoke:

*"God Himself is the great source of power. Furthermore, God's power is available power. We are a supernatural people, born again by a supernatural birth, kept by a supernatural power, sustained by a supernatural Teacher from a supernatural Book. We are led by a supernatural Captain in right paths to assured victories.*

*"The power given is not a gift from the Holy Ghost.* He, Himself, is the power. *Today, He is as truly available and as mighty in power as He was on the day of Pentecost.*

*"It is not lost time to wait upon God."*

Well spoken by a powerful missionary leader.

The most common word for "power" in the Greek

New Testament is *dunamis* (sometimes spelled *dynamis*). However, another Greek work, *energeia*, refers to supernatural energy.

## Monday/Supernatural Energy in the Bible

Supernatural energy is an active power altogether different from physical, mental or emotional energy.

Since supernatural energy is a spiritual reality, why doesn't the Bible say something about it?

It does. The problem lies in the translation from the original Greek language of the New Testament.

Will you put up with another brief Greek lesson? It will help you discover supernatural energy in the Scriptures.

The Greek word translated "energy" in Colossians 1:29 (*NIV, RSV, NEB, TLB*) is *energeia*. Note the similarity to our English word.

The same Greek word is translated "power" in Colossians 2:12 (*NIV, NEB, JB, TEV, Phillips*). Good synonym! In several other places, however, the same Greek noun is translated by the bland English word, "working."[1] Blah!

The *New American Standard Bible* is the most literal word-to-word translation in current English. It most often uses "the working" for *energeia*.[2] That's accurate, but it misses the excitement of supernatural energy.[3]

What's more the word is always used in the New Testament of supernatural beings—either of God or of Satan.[4] It is in fact supernatural energy.

Do understand that I am not questioning the accuracy of our translations of the Bible. I do, however, find that the use of "supernatural energy" instead of "working" makes some Scriptures come alive in a fresh way.

> That power is like the [*supernatural energy*] working
> of his mighty strength which he exerted in Christ
> when he raised him from the dead (Eph. 1:19-20).

> You were also raised up with Him through faith in
> the [*supernatural energy*] working of God, who
> raised Him from the dead (Col. 2:12, *NASB*).

Do you see it? The same supernatural energy that
raised Jesus from the dead is energizing us![5]

When you add the Greek verb, *energeo*, the list of
Scriptures is much longer.[6] For those who like to do their
own Bible word studies, try substituting "supernaturally
energizes" or "supernaturally energizing" for "at work,"
"works" or "working."

> For it is God who [*supernaturally energizes*] works
> in you to will and to act according to his good
> purpose (Phil. 2:13).

So much for the Greek lesson. The point is that God's
supernatural energy is already energizing you to *want to*
fulfill His purposes and to *act* accordingly! That's powerful!
And more of His energy is available! Ask the Holy Spirit to
open the eyes of your heart (Eph. 1:18) so that you may
be enlightened—and supernaturally energized.

---

Pray for enlightenment.
Work for understanding.

## Tuesday/ Evil Energy

Evil energy is running loose in the world.
Anyone can see it—
in the headlines,
in daily life.
Crime, atrocities, conflict, selfishness—somehow
    they keep shocking us.
We tell ourselves this should not be.
It's the exception.
It's in a high crime area.
It's a lack of education or opportunity or
    economic resources.
    Then we discover the same spirit of evil
in our neighborhood,
in our family,
in our own self.
    How can this be? Where does it come from? Why is it
here?
    It's not new. Evil energy did not begin in the twentieth
century or with modern technology or with mass media.
It's been around since the Fall (Gen. 3) and the Bible
answers most of our questions.
    As much as we hate to admit it, we were born with a
bent toward evil. Since every person—except Jesus of
Nazareth—shares this sinful nature, we live in a fallen,
broken world.
    Controlled by the flesh with sinful passions churning
and driving within, it's little wonder that the prophet Jere-
miah cried,

> The heart is deceitful above all things
>     and beyond cure.
> Who can understand it? (Jer.17:9).

Not only is the image of God within every person (Gen. 1:27) warped and distorted, but from without comes the powerful influence of Satan and his demons. The Christian's struggle is *"against the rulers, against the authorities, against the powers of this dark world and against the spiritual forces of evil in the heavenly realms* (Eph. 6:12). In short, we are up against the ranks of the demonic forces.

The devil and his fallen angels, while far less powerful than Christ, do exert an evil energy bent on gratifying sinful desires. Somehow disobedience to God opens a person to this demonic influence. Those who refuse to love the truth and delight in wickedness are sent a powerful delusion to believe Satan's lie (2 Thess. 2:9-11).

And this is not all. Society forms patterns, norms, values that leave God out and bring intense pressure on Christ's followers. *"The ways of this world"* (Eph. 2:2) seem quite acceptable to those who know not Christ.

Add them up.

Driving, draining, warped human passions;
demonic spirits energizing sinful cravings;
world systems excusing and defending
wrongdoing.

What do you get?

An evil energy at work in the world, in every
society, in every neighborhood, in every person.

Evil energy is a bigger problem than we thought.

---

Pray for discernment of evil energy.
Work at claiming Christ's power over it.

## Wednesday/ God's Energizing Word

God's Word supernaturally energizes those who believe. I've seen it again and again.

In high school I was on a Youth for Christ Bible quiz team. With a question-and-answer approach, we studied two books of the New Testament each year. Nine months later we knew what those books said so well that we could finish almost any question on the content and give the answer.

No surprise. This was the fruit of hours of study, practice and drill. The surprise came in the transformed lives of the team members.

Year after year we saw remarkable changes for the better. This was not like studying history and science for a school quiz. It did far more than stimulate young minds.

God's Word, especially when we immersed ourselves in it, made us enthusiastic, committed, on fire for Christ. It had supernatural power.

I saw the same principle at work years later with groups who went through the Bethel Bible Series teacher-training course. For two years each of these groups spent nearly an hour per day apiece studying the Scriptures. Most of the graduates became leaders in the Church. God's Word energized them.

God's Word, when heard and obeyed is living and active (Heb. 4:12). In fact, the original Greek word for "active" means supernaturally energizing.

> For the word of God is living and [*supernaturally energizing*] active (Heb. 4:12).

> The word of God, which is [*supernaturally energizing*] at work in you who believe (1 Thess. 2:13).

Active, at work, energizing—this is the power of God's Word. If you want more supernatural energy, try these ideas.

1. Pray that God will speak to you before you read the Bible, or hear the Scriptures taught or preached. Ask for a responsive spirit and an obedient heart.
2. As you listen or read, open your mind to the Holy Spirit. Expect illumination, insight, even conviction.
3. Mark or jot down what you believe the Holy Spirit said to you. If possible, share it with someone. Take action—worship, love, serve, change, rethink, respond.
4. Bypass excuses for disobeying any part of Scripture. More knowledge never excuses overcoming a struggle in the battleground area of life.
5. Drop defense mechanisms and self-protective behaviors. Allow the Sword of the Spirit, which is the Word of God (Eph. 6:17) to penetrate the thoughts and attitudes of the heart (Heb. 4:12).
6. Revel and rejoice in the sheer privilege of hearing God's Word.

    How sweet are your words to my taste, sweeter than honey to my mouth! (Ps. 119:103).

7. Commune with the living Lord. Ask for His patient, persistent, loving work in building your character and shaping your life. He's faithful and trustworthy!

The law of the Lord is perfect,
   reviving the soul.
The statutes of the Lord are trustworthy,
   making wise the simple.
The precepts of the Lord are right,
   giving joy to the heart.
The commands of the Lord are radiant,
   giving light to the eyes.

—Psalm 19:7-8

> Pray for supernatural energizing.
> Work on obeying God's Word.

## Thursday/ Happy and Unhappy Churches

Supernatural energy flows through God's people. The more joyful the Church, the more people sense God's energy among them.

My friend Ray Ortlund once commented, "There are happy and unhappy churches." He is so right! What makes the difference?

Leadership, wisdom, a spirit of thanksgiving and praise, among other qualities, create a healthy climate. Even more significant is a proper balance of teaching truth and showing love.

Churches who believe all the right things but show little compassion lose their first love and become cold and legalistic (Rom. 2:1-7). Churches who show love but minimize God's revealed truth are warm and accepting but lose their power to convict, convince and deeply transform lives (Rev. 3:14-22).

The apostle Paul strikes the right balance when he writes, "The only thing that counts is faith expressing itself through love" (Gal. 5:6). His formula for growing up into Christ, the Head of the Church, is similar, "speaking the truth in love" (Eph. 4:15).

No church is perfect. What can we do when we discern superficial truth or shallow love in our fellowship?

One of the best strategies is to teach and practice the "one another" commands of the Bible. Some apply to love and others to truth.

| | |
|---|---|
| Love one another. | John 13:34-35; 15:12,17; Rom. 13:8; 1 Thess. 4:9; 1 Pet. 1:22; 1 John 3:11,23; 4:7,11-12; 2 John 5 |
| Be at peace with each other. | Mark 9:50 |
| Be devoted to one another. | Rom. 12:10 |
| Honor one another. | Rom. 12:10 |
| Live in harmony with one another. | Rom. 12:16 |
| Have equal concern for each other. | 1 Cor. 12:25 |
| Serve one another. | Gal. 5:13 |
| Carry each other's burdens. | Gal. 6:2 |

| | |
|---|---|
| Be patient, bearing with one another. | Eph. 4:2; see also Col. 3:13 |
| Be kind and compassionate to one another, forgiving each other. | Eph. 4:32 |
| Submit to one another. | Eph. 5:21 |
| Comfort one another. | 1 Thess. 4:18,*NASB* |
| Encourage one another. | 1 Thess. 5:11; Heb. 10:25 |
| Build each other up. | 1 Thess. 5:11; also see Rom. 14:19 *NASB* |
| Be kind to each other. | 1 Thess. 5:15 |
| Spur one another on toward love and good deeds. | Heb. 10:24 |
| Confess your sins to each other and pray for each other. | Jas. 5:16 |
| Offer hospitality to one another. | 1 Pet. 4:9 |
| Clothe yourselves with humility toward one another. | 1 Pet. 5:5 |

Christ's truth sets people free. That's empowering (John 8:31-32).

Christ's love lifts people's spirits. That's energizing (1 Cor. 8:1).

*"But if we walk in the light, as he is in the light [practice God's truth], we have fellowship with one another [show God's love], and the blood of Jesus, his Son, purifies us from all sin"* (1 John 1:7).

Quality fellowship rooted in truth and love—paves the way for a happy church and a joyful life.

---

Pray for both truth and love in your church.
Work at walking in the light and loving one another.

---

## Friday/ Inspiration

Supernatural energy comes from the Holy Spirit. In chapter nine we will consider this in more detail, but at this point think about how much energy you have when you feel inspired.

Inspiration is an illusive quality. When it's present we feel its lifting effect—creativity, energy, peak performance. When it's absent, we struggle to regain it. At times there seems no way to conjure it up.

As with the Holy Spirit, inspiration is like the wind. We feel its power but do not know where it comes from or where it goes. Inspiration is one form of supernatural energy. Somehow it connects with the image of God stamped deep within every person. It reflects our Lord's own ingenuity and glory.

At times, however, inspiration can turn sour. Just as sin twists and warps the image of God within a person, so inspiration can be bent to evil purposes.

A criminal may get an inspiration to plot a violent crime that escapes detection. Inspiration went wrong. A pastor, on the other hand, may feel inspired to preach a persuasive sermon that draws dozens to Christ. Inspiration went right.

In the original Greek of the New Testament, the word "inspiration" literally means "God-breathed." And God-breathed describes the one sure source of inspiration— the Scriptures. In its highest and best use, inspiration is most plentiful when we draw close to God, His Word and His wonders—love, truth, beauty, creativity, perfection.

God's inspiration often comes to those who aggressively pursue His purposes—seeking Him and serving Him. Wholehearted worship and constant use of one's spiritual gifts pave the way for inspiration.

Inspiration comes with desire. The person who desires a certain goal with enough intensity will often find the inspiration to attain it.

Inspiration comes after prolonged focus. The moment of fresh insight or peak performance follows years of concentration and training.

Inspiration comes with the all-out pursuit of excellence. It seldom comes to those who don't try or don't care.

Inspiration comes with diligence and hard work. J.C. Penney once said that genius was 1 percent inspiration and 99 percent perspiration.

Inspiration often comes after a period of relaxation and refreshment. The rhythm of work and rest produces more creativity or better performance than all of one and none of the other.

Inspiration is contagious. Ball teams, research groups, church choirs, all experience peak periods when together they feel inspired and rise to a higher level than their former best. What results is so good that it brings spontaneous praise from well-informed observers.

If you want inspiration:

- Live close to the God who inspires.
- Associate with inspirational people.
- Join with others to pursue a greater degree of excellence, beauty, knowledge, performance or effectiveness.
- Give it your best shot. Learn from your shortcomings and go after it again.
- Capture the inspirational moment. Learn from it, enjoy it, savor it, praise God for it. Then look for more.
- When inspiration eludes you, substitute perspiration and keep pursuing the goal.
- Never say die. Never give up. Never. Never. Never.

Inspiration is elusive by itself. Give yourself without reservation to God's purpose for your life, however, and it will sneak up on you.

Our Lord likes joyful surprises.

---

Pray for inspiration.
Work with inspiration.

### Saturday/ Why Supernatural Energy?

God gives supernatural energy for His sovereign purposes. He does not give this kind of energy for us to use for selfish reasons—making money, building prestige, getting ahead.
Supernatural energy most often comes for:

1. serving God,
2. seeking God.

When it comes to serving God, spiritual gifts are remarkably energizing. If you have a spiritual gift for teaching, it seems that you can teach all day. If your gift is leadership, you have energy for long meetings that seem to be moving the church or group toward a common goal. If your gift is mercy, you always have the strength to stand by the person who is hurting. God's energy comes with His spiritual gifts for service.

Paul spoke of his great goal, certainly reflecting his own spiritual gifts, just before writing about supernatural energy.

*"We proclaim him [Christ), admonishing and teaching everyone with all wisdom, so that we may present everyone perfect in Christ. To this end I labor, struggling with all his energy, which so powerfully works in me"* (Col. 1:28-29).

Powerful energy from Christ was readily available as the great apostle used his God-given gifts. The same principle applies to us.

If we examine the Bible carefully, we find that supernatural energy is also available for seeking God.

- Moses spent forty days on the mountain with God.
- Jesus fasted for forty days in the wilderness, spent whole nights in prayer, expected His

disciples to "watch" with Him for one hour.

- David prayed at various times in the night or early in the morning.
- Esther considered it normal for herself and her attendants to spend three days fasting and seeking God.

Do you remember when you were engaged? In the height of romantic love, you spent lots of time with your fiance. You may have also been in college or working hard on a demanding job. Yet you had extra energy to spend time—lots of it—enjoying life with your spouse-to-be.

Psychologists tell us that a person in love feels better, is more creative, functions better physically. In short, they have more energy. The same principle operates when Jesus Christ is our first love.

Have you ever noticed that people who spend much time in praise and prayer never complain of fatigue because of it? The Korean Christians are known for rising early every day and gathering in their churches for prayer. Many also spend all night Friday praying together. Yet missionaries report that they are an energetic, hard-working, well-organized people. They have discovered that God gives supernatural energy to seek Him.

Instead of a goal, supernatural energy is better seen as a by-product. When we serve God and seek Christ with all our hearts, He energizes us for the struggle.

Test God and see.

---

Pray to be in tune with God's purposes.
Work at seeking and serving God.

## Sunday/ Discussion Questions

1. Assign the Scriptures in the footnotes for Monday's reading to various ones in your class or group. Substitute "supernatural energy," "energizes" or "energizing" for "works" or "working." It may help to use the *New American Standard Bible*.
2. In each of the Scriptures you read, talk about what God's supernatural energy accomplishes.
3. In your opinion how powerful is evil energy? What are the best defenses against it?
4. Share about the change you saw in yourself or someone you know as a result of applying God's Word. Does more study always bring changes for the better. Why or why not?
5. Do you think your church is better at teaching truth or showing love? Which of the "one another" commands would help most in producing quality fellowship?
6. Have you ever felt inspired with supernatural energy? Describe it. What is the working relationship between inspiration and perspiration.
7. Friday's reading lists several ways to discover or increase inspiration. What others can you think of?
8. Do you agree or disagree that supernatural energy is available only for God's purposes? Can it be abused or misused? Back up your answer with real-life stories.

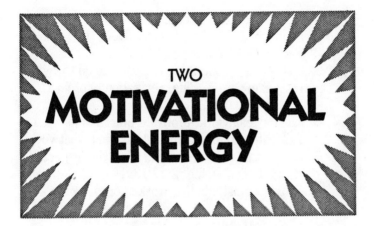

# TWO
# MOTIVATIONAL ENERGY

Motivation is a powerful form of energy.

A motivated person works harder and enjoys it more.

Motivated Christians look to Christ for energy, manage time well and then do everything possible to show love and to lift the morale of those around them.

## Monday/Ten Tips for Time Management

Have you ever said, "There just aren't enough hours in the day"? Have you ever wished for more energy in the hours you do have?

Energy will be wasted unless we use our time well. Here are ten tips that help me and may help you.

1. Begin with Scripture and a prayer: "Lord, take over this day. Take control of every opportunity, conversation, event, encounter, circumstance. Help me in my time, energy, inspiration usage. Make this day all that it should be."

2. Keep your priorities straight. Do your best at

work. Take time to communicate with each member of your family today (Deut. 11:1-21, Eccles. 9:9-10, Matt 6:33).

3. Take time for one thing you want to do today: rest, exercise, reading, recreation, a project, friends (Ps. 90:12).

4. Call for teamwork. Motivate others to join you. Delegate and follow through. It's not what you expect that gets done—it's what you inspect that gets done (Neh. 2:17,18; Neh. 3).

5. Do your most creative work in prime hours when you feel best, think best and create best (Eph. 5:15-16).

6. Make a list of things you need to do. Number them in order of priority. Start with number one and finish each item as you go. Do not worry about what you do not get done, but rejoice in what was finished.

7. Give yourself time limits and deadlines. You can do more in less time when you have to.

8. Schedule in some catch-up times. Without these, you will never get caught up!

9. Keep sensitive to the needs of people around you. No one wants to become a work machine (Luke 10:25-37; Gal. 6:2,5).

10. Consecrate one day a week for worship, rest and doing good to others (Exod. 20:8-11; Eph. 2:8; Heb. 10:24-25).

---

Pray for right priorities.
Work on time management.

## Tuesday/Removing Energy Blocks

It's natural to recoil from pain, including emotional pain. In childhood and youth we learn to protect ourselves. We look for relief when we are embarrassed, humiliated, victimized, isolated, abandoned, disappointed, afflicted or in any way damaged. All of this is natural and normal.

According to Dr. Larry Crabb, this self-protective behavior often creates deeper problems later on.[1] When we adopt *wrong ways* of responding to life's worst experiences we end up building harmful defense mechanisms. These self-protective behaviors can block our perception of God's grace and the flow of supernatural energy.

The basic problem here is not new. It's sin and selfishness. It's all too easy for normal self-protection to degenerate into a sinful blockade of self-giving love. What happens next is that we reject Christ as the deepest answer to our needs and find a selfish substitute instead.

When I look honestly within myself, I find plenty of self-protective behavior that blocks self-giving love.

- I always want to look good in my work and I avoid anything that makes me look bad. This is the exact opposite of laughing at myself and not taking myself too seriously.
- I hold people at arm's length, sometimes cutting them off with "right answers" or legalistic attitudes. This is quite the opposite of exuding warmth and genuine caring—the very love the Bible commands.
- I often deny that circumstances are really bad, especially refusing to *feel* bad about them. (I am unconsciously trying to protect myself from the pain of negative emotions). This is quite the oppo-

site of vulnerable love that weeps with those who weep.

What's radical here is the issue of motives. What looks normal and natural on the surface may hide a selfish and even sinful motive. When our motivation is selfish, our actions—such as attempts to look good—are displeasing to God.

What is the answer? Dr. Crabb recommends that we face up to selfish self-protection as sinful and repent of our wrong motives. Instead of looking to substitute satisfactions for our deepest needs, we place our trust in Christ. He can satisfy the inner thirst, the crucial longings at the core of our being. In the process we must accept and hurt over the fact that some of our less crucial needs will not be fully met until we get to heaven.

When the Holy Spirit cleanses our hearts and motivates us to love Him and others unselfishly, we are on the way to effective change for the better. He begins pushing aside the blocks to supernatural energy. His living water starts flowing from our innermost being.

Jesus Christ meets our deepest needs. In union with Christ we have all the grace (and access to all the energy) that we need to obey His commands.

Even when we hurt.

---

Pray for self-insight.
Work on self-giving love.

## Wednesday/ Esprit de Corps

"The spirit of the group." That's what esprit de corps literally means.

*Webster* defines it as "the common spirit existing in the members of a group and inspiring enthusiasm, devotion and strong regard for the honor of the group."

Some call it high morale. Others call it being filled with the Holy Spirit, living by faith or anticipating God's answers to prayer.

Whatever you call it, esprit de corps makes a powerful impact on people. Think about seven words that build up this illusive quality in the feeling tone of your fellowship.

*Expectancy.* As people come to your church praying and expecting Christ to change someone's life today, the anticipation is contagious. You sense the tone and feel the joy.

*Excitement.* An exciting church usually begins with the spirit of the leaders, paid and unpaid, and spreads to others. It's exciting when good things are happening and relationships are healthy.

*Energy.* Everyone senses the energy that flows from worship. It's especially evident in music and preaching, but also in the nonverbal communication. Smiles, tears, laughter, hushed silence and, yes, sometimes applause.

*Electricity.* When the Holy Spirit moves among us in power and compassion, an "electricity" fills the air. People can sense it better than describe it. The opposite of this feeling is boring, drab, dull and dead. It's totally different than drummed-up enthusiasm or manipulated hype.

*Excellence.* When all that a church, or any group within it, does for the Lord is done first class, with all our might, as unto the Lord, giving it our best shot, prepared and preprayed, then excellence results. People soon sense just how much excellence a church expects and how much it demonstrates.

*Effectiveness.* In the long run there is nothing like effective ministry and service to keep the morale high and the esprit de corps in tip-top shape. Meeting people's needs, worshipful music, helpful preaching and teaching, good leadership, diligent administration, caring concern, hard work, intercessory prayer and the list can go on.

*Eternal results.* Nothing builds esprit de corps in the church like people finding Christ, renewing commitments, turning a corner in their lives and making major break-throughs in their walk with God, marriage, family and ministry.

Sunday worship is a wonderful time to demonstrate these seven good words, and so is the next Sunday, and the next and the next and . . . .

Pray for it.
Work on it.
Prepare for it.
Set the tone for it.
Create the atmosphere for it.
Model it.

Esprit de corps doesn't just happen. It's the dramatic result when all the other qualities mentioned here are in place.

Before you do another thing, prayerfully jot down three things you can do to build the esprit de corps of your church, class or group.

---

Pray for esprit de corps.
Work on expectancy and effectiveness.

---

## Thursday/Excellence

The life of Jesus was marked by excellence!

After one of His wonderful miracles, the people felt overwhelmed with amazement and exclaimed, "He has done everything well" (Mark 7:37).

As resurrected Redeemer, our Lord Jesus continues to do everything well. He excels, and as we live in conscious union with Him, excellence will mark our lives and churches.

Jesus Christ is the head of His Body, the Church, and we are member parts. We excel in obedience to the Scripture and the guidance of the Holy Spirit as our Head gives orders.

Our Lord Jesus is the bridegroom of His bride, the Church. He loves, protects and cherishes us. We excel in loving submission to His overtures as a bride that communes with her bridegroom.

Christ is the architect and builder of His building, the church. We excel in growing in size and perfection of design as our architect and builder does His edifying work.

Our Lord Jesus Christ is the author and finisher of the faith. Since He is the author, we are the book. We excel in holy living and sound doctrine as our author polishes His manuscript.

All of these biblical images of the Church—Christ's Body, bride, building and book—suggest that He is making something special of us. We reflect His handiwork and His image. Because He is excellent, we too excel.

"Ah, how ideal," you say, "but in reality we fall so far short."

Yes, sometimes we do. Yet we must never feel content with what displeases our Lord.

Let us excel in the basics of ministry, like mastering

the fundamentals of a great sport, until our best efforts
show beauty and skill.

Let us excel in concentrating our energy, like an ardent
student studying for an exam until our churches, Sunday
School classes and small groups are willing to apply knowledge and grow.

Let us develop a passion for excellence! Let it be said
of us, *"They have done everything well."*

> Pray for growth.
> Work for excellence.

## Friday/Searching Questions

Peter Drucker is a famous name in management circles.
Author and consultant, this creative and likable man is a
fountain of practical wisdom. Listening to him speak to a
group of Christian leaders and managers in Pasadena, I
picked up a couple of priceless insights. [2]

1. Drucker recommended that every three or four
years, a church or Christian organization take a hard look
at every activity, ministry and service that they offer.
Then ask the first searching question: *If we were not doing
this activity, would we grow into it?* Would the need for it
force us into doing this or something quite similar? Or are
we doing it because of habit, custom or expected program-
ming?

If the answer is, "No, if we did not have this activity or
service, we would *not* grow into it"—then in an organized
way, abandon it. Just drop it—after, of course, finding permission from the governing authorities.

Drucker calls this principle, "intentional abandonment." The great advantage, he says, is that it makes room for innovation. It releases time and energy for something new.

One caution must be heard. This famed management expert warned against dropping areas of great need just because there are not enough qualified people to staff them. Some things are so crucial that we must keep them going in spite of the obstacles.

If you stop to think about it, intentional abandonment can apply to our personal lives and schedules, too. Take a look at your schedule, your commitments, your recreational pursuits. Would you grow into these things if they were abandoned? Are they essential enough to keep pursuing in spite of shortages of time, energy and money?

One key to self-renewal is giving space in our lives for the Holy Spirit to do something fresh and new. This space must be seen in our datebooks and our checkbooks!

2. Once we take the bold step of intentional abandonment and have room for something new, we are ready for the second Drucker insight. He recommended that all managers—leaders, committee chairs, Sunday School department superintendents and so on—take a clean piece of paper and write down the names of each person they supervise who is a consistent performer.

Performers are people who, if you give them a job and they accept it, will always get it done. They always follow through and they do it with excellence.

*Warning*: The first surprise is how few consistent performers you have on the list.

When you recover from this shock, ask the second searching question: *Are consistent performers working on tomorrow?* Are they assigned where there are opportunities or only where there are problems?

Make sure performers are assigned where they can produce! Put them to work in high-yield activities. Turn them loose where they can produce life and growth and not where they are caretakers for deadness. Says Drucker: "There is nothing more futile than trying to keep the corpse from stinking."

On a personal level it pays to ask, "Am I a consistent performer? Do I finish tasks with excellence and with warm relationships intact?"

If the answer is yes, then ask, "'Am I working on tomorrow? Am I spending my time, energy and money on what will count for God's kingdom? Am I investing myself in the life of the Spirit that produces love and growth?"

Searching questions, honest answers and courageous action can lead to self-renewal. Take a moment right now to schedule an hour in your datebook to answer these questions and pray for the Holy Spirit's guidance. It will be worth the time!

---

Pray for discernment.
Work on these searching questions.

---

## Saturday/Turn of Events

High school basketball played a major role in our family for a couple of years. The reason was obvious. My brother, Howard, was one of the starting five for Boise High School.

I recall the playoff game with our arch rival, Borah High. With three minutes to play, our team's score lagged seventeen points behind. The fans on our side were unusually quiet and dispirited, some had already left the gymnasium. Losing—especially losing by a big margin—is no fun.

To make matters worse, Bobby, one of our players, lost his temper at the referee. The ref not only called a technical foul, he kicked Bobby out of the game. To his team members, the penalty seemed too severe for the infraction. But somehow it sparked fire in them.

All at once our Boise team turned red-hot and began playing their best. Borah turned icy cold and kept losing the ball. It seemed that Fred, the leading scorer, and my brother, Howard, simply could not miss. They began sinking outside shots, over and over—and the score narrowed.

Borah suffered turnover after turnover. The Boise High crowd, once subdued, went wild. We cheered and yelled and screamed like I seldom recall in my life. The score kept getting closer and closer as the clock ticked away.

In the final seconds, Howard sank a long shot that put us one point ahead. We went wild with joy. Borah never regained the lead.

Turn of events. What a difference in morale and energy a deeply desired turnaround can make.

It was the day following the crucifixion of Jesus. His disciples observed the Sabbath in the customary Jewish way during the day. Grief plunged its icy fingers into their hearts.

As evening fell, ending the Sabbath, people poured into the streets to socialize—a usual Jewish custom. Not the apostles. They huddled together behind locked doors, afraid.

Jesus was crucified and buried. Were they next? How

far would their enemies go in their efforts to stop this new movement?

A second day passed, and on the third, strange things began to happen. Mary Magdalene reported that someone had moved the body of Jesus. A confirmation came from Peter and John that the tomb was empty, although the grave clothes were still in place. Cleopas and his companion showed up, all excited, claiming they had talked with Jesus.

The score was changing; despair was turning to perplexity. Would our team make a comeback?

Before they could sort through all the emotions, Jesus appeared in their midst. It was the final seconds of the game and He made the winning basket. Despair turned to joy.

A dramatic turn of events can lift morale and give fresh enthusiasm. All by itself, however, the sudden win is not enough. It takes a winning season, not just a single game, to keep a team on top.

Over a period of forty days, Jesus gave many convincing proofs that He was resurrected. After touching Him, eating with Him, listening to what He said about the Kingdom of God, watching the miraculous ascension into the clouds above, the disciples were fully convinced.

They waited, prayed, obeyed His command to stay in Jerusalem. At the feast of Pentecost the Holy Spirit came upon them with enabling power and miraculous signs. They were never the same again.

From defeat and despair to hope and joy, what a turn of events. No basketball game could compare.

When you feel like a loser, when your team is far behind, when a key player is knocked out of the game, don't give up. A divine turn of events can turn your sorrow into joy!

The turnaround victory has already been won! Our Best Player is back in the game! During this last three minutes on history's clock every shot counts.

Play your best!

---

Pray for a turn of events.
Work at giving it your best.

---

## Sunday/ Discussion Questions

1. In your opinion what motivates people in a way that energizes them?
2. Share your best insight into improving time management. (I love the man who said, "Retire!")
3. Plan to ask your best friend, spouse or parents what your self-protective behaviors are. What do you expect them to say?
4. Take a three-by-five card. On one side write, "Self-protective Behaviors" at the top. List all you can think of and also those items mentioned by those who love you most (see question 3 above). On the other side of the card write "Self-giving Love." List the opposite loving response that might replace each self-protective behavior. Keep this card as a prayer/action guide.
5. Much of our Christian life is related to churches, classes and groups. In your discussion, ask each person to jot down three things that can be done to build esprit de corps. Combine your lists and talk about it.
6. Under what circumstances is the pursuit of excellence

a Christ-centered activity and under what circumstances is it a manipulative tool used by leaders to attain their own goals?
7. With the officers of your church, class or group, ask Peter Drucker's two searching questions. Discuss the answers together.

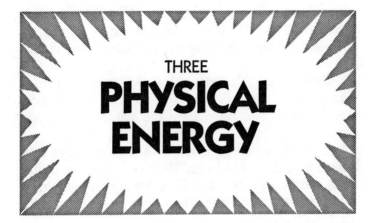

# THREE
# PHYSICAL ENERGY

God cares about our human bodies. His written Word holds some practical instructions regarding physical energy.

Since our bodies and spirits affect each other, it's only smart to pay attention to the physical. This week we will look at some tips for building nonsupernatural human energy.

## Monday/**Purifying the Body**

Christianity takes the human body seriously. It's worthy of respect, care and, ultimately, resurrection.

Some Eastern religions put all the emphasis on the soul and *"spiritual experience."* They either punish the body in rigorous self-denial or indulge bodily desires, considering the flesh passing and unimportant.

Modern pagans almost worship the body, making a

near-cult out of physical beauty. The *"beautiful people"* are admired, pictured in the media and put on display as models. No wonder many others feel inferior and undervalued.

Christianity has a better idea. Our heavenly Father created our human bodies, male and female, and put us in a holy relationship. We possess the stamp of His image upon us (Gen. 1:27).

Our Lord Jesus Christ became a real man with a fully human body. Born of a virgin, He lived with all the limitations of homo sapiens. Then He suffered bodily pain, died a physical death and was raised again in a resurrected, immortal body.

The Holy Spirit lives within the body of every Christian, indwelling us as His temple (1 Cor. 6:19). The body of every born-again believer is the very sanctuary of God (1 Cor. 3:16).

Ah, now we get to the point. Since our bodies are sacred to God, He asks us to purify them (2 Cor. 7:1).

What would it take to purify your body?

- Weight loss?
- Regular exercise?
- Enough sleep?
- Relaxed vacation?
- Improved diet?
- Weekly fasting?
- Physical check-up?
- Stop smoking?
- Quit drinking?
- Say no to drugs?
- Sexual control?

All of these, and more, are important to God! He wants to live in a body yielded to Him without reservation (Rom. 12:1).

There is more. The Bible puts a special emphasis on offering the parts of our body to God to live out a life of righteousness (Rom. 6:11-13).

- The thoughts of our brain
- The expressions on our face
- The touch of our hands
- The words of our mouth
- The direction of our feet

So important is this commitment to Christ that when we stand before His judgment seat (in a resurrected body, by the way), we will get what is due us for *"the things done while in the body, whether good or bad"* (2 Cor. 5:10).

The first step toward bounding energy—and a life pleasing to God-is to purify ourselves from everything that contaminates the body.

Take inventory. Ask the Holy Spirit where He wants to begin the repair and refurbishing of His temple, your body (1 Cor. 6:19-20; 2 Cor. 6:16-7:1).

Your body is important to God!

---

> Pray for physical energy.
> Work at purifying your body.

---

## Tuesday/Fit or Fat?

Physical exercise is a funny thing.

It takes too much time. Unless, of course, it's done regularly. Then it creates its own time.

Consistent aerobic exercise reduces the need for sleep by about the same amount of time as it requires. Thirty minutes each day of continued exercise, for example, reduces the need for sleep by about a half hour per night.

"Aerobic" simply describes exercise that keeps the heart and lungs moving at a given level for fifteen minutes to an hour. In his helpful book, *Fit or Fat?* Covert Bailey suggests a minimum of twelve minutes per day.[1] A half hour every other day is second choice.

The right kind and amount of exercise will burn excess fat. It doesn't replace a healthy diet but it makes losing weight, especially shuffling off fat, so much easier. The body metabolism actually changes to consume extra fat instead of storing it.

To turn a body from a fat-storage machine into a fit temple of the Holy Spirit requires a key of knowledge— and using it. The key is to find that right heart rate for prolonged exercise that burns fat rather than builds fatigue.

A simple formula is to subtract one's age from one hundred and eighty. For example, at this writing I am forty-seven years old. So $180-47=133$. If I jog, swim, row, stairstep, jump rope, walk vigorously or ride a bike so that my heart rate stays close to one hundred thirty-three (10 percent above or below) for fifteen minutes a day or thirty minutes every other day—I am exercising aerobically.

One simple way to check my heartbeat is to pause and immediately take my pulse for six seconds. Then multiply by ten. This method is close enough to accuracy and does not seriously disrupt exercising. Another way is to purchase a pulse watch at a sports store.

I have experienced my own set of objections to consistent aerobic exercise. Maybe you can relate.

- *I don't like how tired it makes me.*
  If I keep at it for enough weeks, sure enough, it becomes energizing. Tiredness turns to mild exhilaration. I actually have more energy in a given week than if I miss the discipline.

- *I don't like the sore muscles.*
  Yet if I keep it up, in a couple of weeks the
  soreness is gone. Then my body tones up. I feel
  better and can go longer and harder. Mild
  stress—even physical—builds strength.
- *I don't like the boredom of endless repetition.*
  Unless, of course, I use these moments
  creatively. Praising, praying, quoting Scripture
  add spiritual benefit. Good thinking or rest from
  thinking adds mental energy.
- *I would prefer team sports with competition.*
  This is an objection I hear from others. Since I am
  short on athletic ability, aerobic exercise works
  best for me. Team sports certainly have their
  benefits—friendship, fellowship, character
  building, teamwork, witnessing opportunities, and
  so on. Physical fitness experts warn that they
  may not burn fat as well as consistent aerobic
  exercise.

I sometimes wonder why the Bible says so little about
physical exercise. Certainly it gives priority to getting in
shape spiritually. Maybe it's because people *walked* everywhere. The hours of walking, sometimes carrying loads,
provided a built-in aerobic exercise system. It's interesting
to note the Bible's references to walking with God and to
God walking (exercising) with His people (Gen. 17:1; Lev.
26:12; and others).

*"Train yourself to be godly,"* writes the apostle Paul.
*"For physical training is of some value, but godliness has
value for all things, holding promise for both the present life
and the life to come"* (1 Tim. 4:7-8).

He's right. Physical exercise does not bring the same
profit as training in holy living. But it does help some. The

person who wants more energy will welcome it.

> Pray for discipline.
> Work at removing excuses.

## Wednesday/Too Much Sleep?

The Bible chides the workaholic who cheats himself on sleep in order to make another buck: *"In vain you rise early and stay up late, toiling for food to eat—for he grants sleep to those he loves"* (Ps. 127:2).

In perfect balance, the Word of God makes fun of the person who sleeps too much: *"A little sleep, a little slumber, a little folding of the hands to rest—and poverty will come on you like a bandit and scarcity like an armed man"* (Prov. 24:33-34).

In harsher tones, God warns: *"Do not love sleep or you will grow poor; stay awake and you will have food to spare"* (Prov. 20:13).

Is it possible to sleep too much? Can we sleep less, feel just as good, accomplish more and not hurt ourselves?

For many people the answer to these questions is a resounding, yes.

On vacation I can sleep nine hours every night. Why not? I have the time and enjoy the relaxation.

The rest of the year I function well on seven hours sleep per night, sometimes less. The difference, obviously, is two hours per day.

The exact amount of sleep needed varies, but the point is that most people can function well on less than their maximum sleep capability.

What could you do with two more hours per day, or even one, or a half hour? What if you spent it in prayer or worship or Bible study? What if you gave it to outreach ministry? What if you shared it with your family?

To reduce your sleep and increase your effectiveness try a few simple experiments:

Try setting your alarm for fifteen minutes earlier than you normally get up. Leave it at that spot for several days, even a week or two. If you function well, once you adjust, set it back another fifteen minutes. Keep this up until you find the right sleep level for maximum productivity.

Try going to bed earlier. Late hours spent before the TV often profit little. Early hours spent with the Lord profit much.

Try a twenty-minute nap during the day. Sleep experts (and short-nap lovers) know that this revitalizes energy. The key is to set an alarm so you don't sleep too long. All that is needed is enough time to doze off. Long naps slow down the system so much that they only produce a better feeling the next day.

Try making the Lord's Day—or your day off if you are a pastor—a real day of worship and rest. God made us to rest one day in seven. We violate ourselves when we ignore His built-in laws.

Sleep less. Rest more. Feel better. Enjoy the Lord and His life.

This calls for careful balance, but the wise Christian will find it.

> Pray for inner calm.
> Work at creative rest.

## Thursday/ Too Little Sleep?

I have written about too much sleep. To give balance, I want to address the other side of the issue.

"Burning the candle at both ends," as the old saying goes, is a way of life for many overstressed people. Remember that the psalmist is right when he chides, *"In vain you rise early and stay up late, toiling for food to eat— for he grants sleep to those he loves"* (Ps. 127:2).

Too little sleep leaves our adrenalin level too high. In his insightful book, *Adrenalin and Stress*, Dr. Archibald Hart shows the effect that sleep has on restoring our bodies.[2] Relief from stress with its deadly damage comes hard when there is a lack of sleep and exercise.

Too little sleep cuts into our creativity. It's possible to function on less sleep but at the sacrifice of those times of spontaneous insight that make job, family and church more effective and enjoyable.

Too little sleep produces fatigue. In the long run, fatigue takes its toll in discouragement, depression or burnout. Negative emotions thrive on fatigue.

Too little sleep curbs our efficiency. A tired worker seems to exert himself as much as anyone else, but the results are far less productive.

Too little sleep does physical harm to the body. Each person needs a certain amount of dreaming and a certain amount of nondream rest in each twenty-four hour period. When deprived of this the physical body and mental energy suffer.

So what is a busy person supposed to do?

*Reevaluate your attitude.* Life is a relay race. We carry the baton only part way before passing it on to others. Holding on to the baton too long is just as destructive as turning loose of it too quickly.

*Go to bed earlier.* It's possible to get as much news reading the paper standing up for five minutes the next morning as in thirty minutes of TV at eleven P.M. the night before. Set up bedtime fifteen minutes per week until you feel rested and relaxed.

*Relax.* Even five minutes of relaxation once or twice a day can refresh body and spirit. Prayer, Scripture meditation and plain, old rest are minibreaks that help.

*Keep in tune with your body.* One early riser I know simply puts his head down on his desk when he feels tired. Sometimes he dozes off. This man has incredible energy that amazes even his family. Headaches, drowsiness, fatigue symptoms most often suggest the need for rest rather than the need for painkillers such as aspirin or Tylenol.

*Exercise regularly.* Regular aerobic exercise every day or two—the kind that keeps the heart and lungs working for twenty to thirty minutes—burns off excess adrenalin, stimulates natural painkillers in the brain and reduces the need for extra sleep. Exercise makes its own time.

*Take a day off every week.* God built the human body for one day of rest out of seven. Ignore the Sabbath principle to your own peril. Funny, isn't it, that people who work six days and rest one get even more done than those who work seven in a row—or work five and wear themselves out with other activities for two more.

Too much sleep or too little? Evaluate yourself and ask the Lord to make you a good steward of your time.

---

Pray for good judgment.
Work at finding the right sleep pattern.

## Friday/ High-energy Food

I grew up a meat-and-potatoes man. Or, better yet, fried chicken with mashed potatoes and gravy and fresh corn on the cob.

I never heard talk about cholesterol or high-energy foods. But my grandpa dropped dead of a heart attack at age 65. My aunt died of heart problems even younger. My uncle survived a major coronary.

Today more of us than ever are conscious of food, diet, health and energy. More and more of us are finding from our own experience that replacing sugars and fats with carbohydrates and noncholesterol proteins makes us feel better and look good.

A healthy diet, including less caffeine and no alcohol or drugs, produces a more energetic body. Less sickness and a longer life span are predictable fringe benefits.

What does the Bible say about food?

The Seventh-Day Adventists pick up on the Old Testament dietary regulations. The strict ones are vegetarians. The studies show that indeed they live longer than other groups. They claim to be healthier, too.

As a matter of personal choice, I can respect their teaching, but do not agree with their interpretation of God's commands. The New Testament, which fulfills the Old Testament, clearly gives freedom concerning food (Mark 7:19; Rom. 14:14; 1 Cor. 8:8; 10:25-26,31).

The Bible warns about the dangers of gluttony (Prov. 23:19-21; 28:7) but this vice does not appear in the New Testament with drunkenness and the list of sins of those who will not inherit the kingdom of God (1 Cor. 6:9-10; Gal. 5:19-21; 1 Pet. 4:3-5).

In contrast to gluttony, fasting is often commended. This is especially true when its purpose is to enhance prayer rather than to earn points with God (Matt. 6:16-18; Mark 2:18-20; Acts 13:2-3; 14:23).

I recall my shock when a seminar speaker told about confronting a person who was grossly overweight. Somehow the subject of being filled with the Holy Spirit came up. As I recall, the speaker said pointedly, "The Holy Spirit would not live in your body. It's an unfit temple for Him!"

I believe the speaker went too far, but his basic thought still intrigues me. As Christians, our bodies *are* temples of the Holy Spirit (1 Cor. 6:19-20). Should we not treat them with as much respect and care as the church building where we worship? This certainly includes healthy food.

Want more physical energy? Pursue a balanced, healthy diet. Add one day a week of fasting. Check your energy level in three or four months and see if you don't feel better.

It's worth a try.

---

Pray for good health.
Work at eating right.

---

### Saturday/ The Resurrected Body

The apostle Paul—as throughout the New Testament—does not pretend to know fully what the future resurrection body is like (1 Cor. 15:35-58; Phil. 3:20-21; I John 3:2). The one thing that is certain is that it will be like the resurrected body of our Lord Jesus Christ. This is enough to know.

However, under the inspiration of the Holy Spirit, the apostle gives one fascinating insight.

*"So will it be with the resurrection of the dead. The body that is sown is perishable,* . . . *it is sown in dishonor,*. . . *it is raised in power, it is sown a natural body, it is raised a spiritual body"* (1 Cor. 15:42-44).

Will you put up with a brief Greek lesson?

The Greek word for "natural" body is *psychikon.* It literally means "natural" or "physical." It also implies something more.

Our word "psychic" comes from this Greek root. This present body is an organ of the psyche, our emotional/mental make-up.

We understand the term *"psychosomatic."* It is a bodily disorder that is influenced by a psychic or emotional cause. The body and mind interact. Emotions affect our glandular systems, immune systems and nervous systems.

Contrast this with the word for "spiritual" body, *pneumatikon.* The Greek word *pneuma* means "spirit." It can refer to either the human spirit or the Holy Spirit.

Our present body responds to our psychic/emotional/mental make-up. It does not respond as well to our human spirit.

The resurrected *pneumatikon* body, the spiritual body, will respond to our spiritual make-up. It will be fully in tune with the Holy Spirit. All of its systems will receive stimuli from the human spirit and the Spirit of God and respond accordingly.

Have you ever wanted to pray, but felt so sleepy you could hardly stay awake? Have you ever wanted to understand God's written Word but just couldn't concentrate? Have you ever wanted to worship but your throbbing headache ruined it? Your *psychikon* body was standing in the way of your spirit's desires.

How glorious it will be to have a body that fully responds to God and the highest desires of our own spirit. I imagine that when we want to pray or worship our body will become alert, energized, ready, receptive to God. Our concentration, emotions and awareness will immediately be activated for the working of the Holy Spirit.

Our whole life in the *pneumatikon* body will be adapted to the "new heavens and the new earth," our new environment. It will be powerful, indestructible and glorious.

It will not, however, be just a disembodied spirit floating around the clouds of heaven. New Testament scholar, Dr. George Eldon Ladd, wrote: "A spiritual body is by no means a body made out of spirit, any more than a natural (*psychikos*) body is a body made out of psyche."[3]

So much for the Greek. Think for a moment what it might be like to enjoy a body infused with the life-giving Spirit of God.

Will we communicate perfectly in it?

Will we understand each other fully in it?

Will we enjoy the beauty of heaven in it?

Will we explore the universe in it?

Will we grasp the majesty and glory of God in it?

My guess is that the answer to all these questions is a resounding yes.

I am looking forward to a resurrected, *pneumatikon* body. How about you?

---

Pray for patience with your *pschikon* body.
Work at anticipating your *pneumatikon* body.

## Sunday/Discussion Questions

1. What would it take to purify your body? What now defiles it? See 2 Cor. 7:1. Check the list under Monday's reading and select one to work on.
2. What are some common excuses for avoiding exercise? What are yours?
3. Are you getting too much or too little sleep?
4. Some people seem fanatical about "eating right." Others only care about what tastes good. In your opinion, what is the healthy balance between these two viewpoints?
5. Most people think of Christianity as dealing with spiritual things. Why do you think the Bible has so much to say about the human body?
6. What would it take to make the Lord's Day a time of Sabbath rest? How would your family life change if worship and relaxation were priorities *every* Sunday?
7. Discuss the limitations of our present *psychikon* bodies. How do you think our future *pneumatikon* bodies will be different? Does this increase your anticipation of heaven?

# FOUR
# ENERGY DRAINERS

Trouble,
　discouragement,
　　fatigue,
　　　anger,
　　　　procrastination,
　　　　　job dissatisfaction
　　　　　　and a dozen other energy drainers can sap
　　　　　　our strength and reduce our power.

Supernatural energy works best when we need God most—in the strain of the struggle.

Ignore energy drainers and end up exhausted and empty. Fail to deal with them and, like a hole in the dam, energy spills into counterproductive and even destructive torrents of wastedness.

Face up to them, calling upon Christ's supernatural energy, and find strength for the struggle.

## Monday/ Hard Times

No one goes through life without facing hard times.

Tragedy, suffering, pain and sorrow cause us to cry out to God! A marriage without romance, a divorce in the family, conflict in the home, unhappiness on the job, a financial squeeze on the pocketbook, a betrayal by a loved one and much, much more drain us and drive us to Him.

I am learning, or relearning, a couple of simple lessons in the hard times.

Here's one. **God is just as faithful in the hard times as He is in the good times.**

True, most adults who accept Christ come to Him out of a sense of need. Equally true, much of our Christian maturity comes through the beatings and blows of circumstances against the anvil of life. In the toughest times— when we feel victimized, stressed out, snubbed or forgotten—the Lord remains faithful.

Here's a second and more painful lesson. **Hard times show up flaws within me that I did not know were there.**

Under pressure or emotional strain, I sometimes react in ways that are far less Christian than I like to think about myself. Once the character defect shows up, then I have to deal with it before the Lord:

Sometimes I must repent of my action and ask forgiveness of someone I have hurt.

Sometimes I must change a deep-seated attitude.

Sometimes I must alter an ingrained habit pattern.

Sometimes I must develop a new character quality.

These all sound fine until they become specific. Bridling my tongue, restraining my anger, purifying my thoughts, loving my enemies seem next to impossible in real life.

*Impossible* is what God specializes in, and so I run to Him. He brings comfort for my hurts, motivation to change, power to move toward Christlikeness and wisdom in dealing with irregular people.

The Bible even says that we can "exult in our tribulations" (Rom. 5:3 *NASB*) and "consider it pure joy" (Jas. 1:2) when we face trials of many kinds. That sounds like a slap in the face when going through the hard times—unless we also look at the rewards. Perseverance, maturity, character, completeness, hope. These are the makings of a likeable person and a powerful Christian.

Mileage out of misery, melody out of malady, stumbling-blocks into stepping-stones, joy over tears, triumph over trouble, life over death—in short, it's Christ over crud.

> I walked a mile with Pleasure,
> she chattered all the way;
> But left me none the wiser
> For all she had to say.

> I walked a mile with Sorrow,
> And ne'er a word said she;
> But, oh, the things I learned from her
> When sorrow walked with me. [1]

Looking back, hard times are sometimes the best times.

---

Pray for relief.
Work on rejoicing in Christ,
even in the hard times.

## Tuesday/ Dealing with Discouragement

An old legend (with some changes) says that the devil once put his flaming arrows up for sale (Eph. 6:16). Lust, pride, gossip, resentment, greed and deceit were all reasonably priced. One well-worn but extremely fiery dart was set apart on display by itself. The price was astronomical.

*"That's discouragement,"* commented the devil. *"With it I pierce the emotions of almost every Christian. It wounds many people, forcing them to want to give up. It's my number one weapon in fighting against God's progress."*

Rumor has it that the price was so high that no one bought this flaming missile. Satan pulls it from his arsenal daily and fires it into the hearts of some of Christ's finest warriors.

Of all the attacks of the evil one, discouragement is one of the most debilitating. It saps energy, puts a person on the brink of depression, and slows down God's work.

The first cousin of discouragement is self-pity. It's second cousin is lethargy. It's third cousin is named "Quitter."

Certain circumstances make almost everyone susceptible to an attack of discouragement.

- Fatigue
- Malicious criticism
- Unresolved conflict
- Quiet but stubborn opposition
- Absence of caring energetic support

What's easy to miss is that the brother of discouragement is opportunity. The very circumstances that disheartened some will lead others to show remarkable leadership. Think about these seven principles for dealing with discouragement.

1. *Get enough rest.* Physical, emotional and spiritual rest (Heb. 4) are essentials for coping with discouraging times. Ignore adequate time for recovery after high stress periods and your whole system will break down.
2. *Find a close friend who will stand by you.* A listening ear, a compassionate heart, some encouraging words can make all the difference when you are discouraged.
3. *Let God fight for you.* Christ has the solution and the resources to turn discouraging circumstances into remarkable answers to prayer. Fervently seek Him.
4. *Balance faith with caution.* Seek wise counsel from those in authority over you and from Christians you trust and respect. Others have overcome similar problems and circumstances. Find out how the winners did it.
5. *Call for all the help you can get.* More people are willing to help than you may imagine. Call on intercessors, encouragers, motivators, volunteer workers, financial supporters and whoever else is needed.
6. *Get back to work.* Resolve the conflict, answer the critics, heal the wounded, fix the problem, apply the solution, motivate the lethargic, take action. Then learn to live with less than perfection or idealism. God measures success by faithfulness and obedience, not results.
7. *Rally around a great cause.* Move to a high spiritual plane, challenging yourself and others to

excel for Christ, even in these discouraging circumstances.

What if you follow all these principles, and nothing much changes?

No matter what others do or don't do, no matter how great the problems, no matter what the outcome of circumstances, you can pursue maturity in Christ and become a better person.

*"Therefore put on the full armor of God, so that when the day of evil comes, you may be able to stand your ground, and after you have done everything, to stand. Stand firm then"* (Eph. 6:13-14).

*"He who stands firm to the end will be saved"* (Matt. 24:13; Mark 13:13)

Discouragement need not do you in. Deal with it in Christ's power and you will become an overcomer.

---

> Pray for encouragement.
> Work on perseverance.

---

## Wednesday/ Halfway-Point Fatigue

Beware of the fatigue that strikes just after the halfway point of any project.

When a job is about half done, fatigue sets in. The excitement of starting has worn off and what's left is a job that looks impossible to finish.

Starting is half done, but finishing is the tougher half. Many a football team that is leading at the half loses the game in the third quarter. Many a seminar speaker discovers that the hardest time to hold people's attention and arouse enthusiasm is from 1-3 P.M., halfway through the day. Many a student lets up on his studies and fouls up his grade in the course just after midterm finals. Many a church finds that the greatest resistance to recruiting more volunteer workers on a new building takes place when the project is half finished.

Halfway is a predictable low point. We feel tired, worn out, discouraged, disheartened. "Can't" talk begins. "I can't take it anymore." "We can't keep this up."

Self-pity follows. We focus on the problems, and too often exaggerate them. Like noticing a black smudge on a white shirt, we see only the negative.

The rumor mill swings into action. Criticism of the leader makes the rounds. The reported comments of the gripers are passed from person to person. All of this started with the fatigue that predictably comes at the halfway point.

So what can be done?

*Schedule a break ahead of time.* Schools give a semester break halfway through the academic year. Football games schedule halftime for rest and the proverbial coach's pep talk. Some cultures plan an afternoon siesta. Even in ours a short rest or nap often helps.

*Set the pace in caring for the burned-out.* Face up to the reality of fatigue and its energy-sapping power. Show compassion and understanding to those who suffer.

*Plan a motivator for halftime.* Awards, encouragement, pats on the back, corrective counsel, addressing the problems, answering the rumors—all are vital.

*Refocus on the original purpose.* Find the original reason the project was important enough to start, and talk about progress toward this goal. Focus on God's purpose in it.

*Bring in fresh reinforcements.* New volunteers, new players, new resources, new hired help all give a boost to everyone's morale.

*Move ahead in faith.* When dealt with properly, fatigue is temporary. See it as one hurdle, not the end of the race.

Halfway-point fatigue is predictable. Don't let it catch you by surprise.

> Pray for renewed excitement.
> Work at preplanned pacing.

### Thursday/ Watch Out for Anger!

*"My dear brothers, take note of this: Everyone should be quick to listen, slow to speak and slow to become angry, for man's anger does not bring about the righteous life that God desires"* (Jas. 1:19-20).

Anger—deep, strong and difficult to hide—is one of the most troublesome of emotions. It pops up with a dozen faces. Consider a few:

- *Belligerence*: glaring eye, scowl, broken or loud speech, storm out of room, slam doors, drawers, books.
- *Contrariness*: irritability, "steaming," grumpiness, bigotry, racism, getting even, taking it out on someone else.
- *Excessive Politeness*: overconsideration of the one who is annoying, phony courtesy, "shining him on."
- *Withdrawal*: depression, brooding, sulking, pouting, indifference.

Anger comes as a reflex to any blow that damages inner prestige, as a reaction to a loss of invincibility. It's a kissing cousin of frustration, the emotion that mounts when a barrier stands between us and solving our problems.

To cool anger in others, the Bible says, *"A gentle answer turns away wrath"* (Prov. 15:1).

The Bible urges us to be *"slow to anger"* (Prov. 16:32; Jas. 1:19). It holds us responsible for what we do with our anger (Matt. 5:21-22). It commands us to release our anger before the sun goes down (Eph. 4:26).

The best solution is to replace or redirect anger. The Holy Spirit within us can give us the power to *"put away"* this destructive feeling and *"put on"* Jesus Christ and His rich character qualities of patience, gentleness, compassion and joy. As this bit of doggerel says,

Anger burns, churns, spurns.

Jesus cools fools with His rules.

Take your pick.

---

Pray for gentleness—power under control.
Work on becoming slow to anger.

---

## Friday/ Procrastination

I wanted to write about procrastination today—but I didn't have quite enough time.

Does anyone besides me ever feel guilty for procrastinating?

I know that sometimes it's good to procrastinate.

("Hesitate" is a better word). "Planned procrastination" is a proven time-management principle. *"Always put off until tomorrow the things that you shouldn't do at all,"* quipped Frances Rodman[2].

However, if procrastination causes you pain. If putting things off gets you in trouble. If you're always under the pile,

> behind the eight ball,
> swamped,
> burned out,
> panic stricken over deadlines,

then there is good news for you.

Christ can help you whip procrastination.

I am not trying to put a guilt trip on those who are already doing their reasonable best. Special understanding goes to the mothers of young children, those who are working three jobs and struggling to survive, those who are in college or graduate school with an extra-heavy academic load.

For most of us procrastination is either a paralyzing feeling or a deadly habit.

The feeling comes when a certain job or project is hanging over our heads. We either can't get started or don't get back to what we have already started.

A gnawing feeling on the inside keeps us from completely forgetting it. We make excuses, feel guilty, get an uneasy sensation in the pit of our stomachs. Yet we can't seem to get moving on it, nor can we forget it and enjoy something else.

Panic rises as the deadline approaches. Instead of giving it extra effort, we freeze. We look for ways to delay without losing face.

In the end we work around the clock, settle for a "quicky" shortcut, or miss the deadline with a well-rehearsed apology. We tell ourselves that *never* again will we go through this—until next time.

If you are sometimes plagued with procrastination, consider these tips (please do not procrastinate putting them into practice):

- Start now.
- Earnestly ask the Lord's guidance before accepting an assignment.
- Eliminate and concentrate.
- Undercommit rather than overcommit.
- Never promise more than you can deliver.
- Be vicious with time-wasters.
- Set aside forty-five minutes to do fifteen little things that take three minutes or less.
- Fix your eye on one goal, and reach it.
- Refocus your priorities.
- Keep pace with the Lord.

> Pray for early diligence.
> Work at promptness.

## Saturday/ The Flatter Platter

Many Christians feel frustrated with their job and do not understand why.

It's not the overall career they hate. Nor is it that they can't work well with people. They function well in the assigned tasks and managers seem pleased, but on the inside those frustrated workers are dying. They are capable of so much more.

Feelings swing back and forth. At times they feel unappreciated, overlooked, undervalued. They are convinced that they could do a better job if promoted one or two levels and paid accordingly.

At other times they feel worthless and wonder if they are going crazy. The evaluation of those around them must be correct after all! They feel trapped in the present position, self-deluded with visions of grandeur.

According to Christian personnel psychologist Dr. Dan Smith, these feelings are common for someone with a "tipped platter."

Picture a large round platter in your mind. Job satisfaction and career development depend on three things staying in balance. Visualize three strands or supports holding up the platter. If all three are at the same level, the platter is flat, symbolizing job satisfaction. If they are at different heights, the platter tips and the food slides off. Career development is out of whack.

The three axis are:

> the job—easy or difficult,
> the compensation—high or low,
> the ability—much or little.

First, the *job* itself needs to challenge the person to grow and develop without that uneasy feeling that it's too much. Like a rubber band, the tasks need to stretch the worker, but not so much that it breaks.

Second, the *compensation* needs to be fair for this job. Many pastors, for example, are grossly underpaid. Their skills, problem-solving abilities and hours worked would garnish them double or triple their income in secular work.

Dr. Smith suggests that a "20 percent Christian discount is reasonable" but a 100 percent or more discount is unjust and unfair. Far too many pastors and their spouses are suffering severe financial pressure that they do not feel free to talk about.

Money is not the only factor. Nonmonetary compensation—praise, recognition, working conditions, warm relationships, high morale—are even more important.

Third, the *ability* of the worker needs to match the assigned tasks. Growth in skill, brain power and problem-solving capability creates an inner demand for assignments that use these abilities. However, if a person gets placed in a job that demands too much ability, frustration and failure will follow.

What's a person with a tipped platter supposed to do? Only a few options exist. Consider one or two of the following.

- Appeal for a job review that takes these factors into account. Talk with bosses or managers about "job fit."
- Change jobs to one that provides a flatter platter.
- Use gifts, abilities, strengths and skills in church and voluntary organizations in a way that produces inner satisfaction.
- For personal, family or financial reasons, stay where you are and accept living with the frustration. Appeal to Christ to meet your deepest needs and to open up reasonable opportunities to flatten your platter.

Bosses and managers, pastors and church leaders hold a special opportunity to assess the job, the compensation and the ability of each worker. More than others they have the authority to create a flatter platter. What an opportunity for Christian service!

Under the inspiration of the Holy Spirit, Paul writes, *"Serve wholeheartedly, as if you were serving the Lord, not men, because you know that the Lord will reward everyone for whatever good he does"* (Eph. 6:7-8).

Let's give one another a flatter platter—and look for the Lord's rewards.

> Pray for a flatter platter.
> Work at honest self-evaluation.

## Sunday/ Discussion Questions

1. Share the hardest time you ever faced. How has Christ helped you deal with that memory?
2. How do you overcome discouragement? Is it possible to avoid it altogether?
3. What effect does fatigue have on our outlook? How can we learn to pace ourselves when so many unexpected things happen?
4. What practical steps make you "slow to become angry"? As Christians, how can we become more honest in facing up to our anger? Is it ever a virtue to hide anger?
5. Name some excuses that people use to justify "putting it off." How would you suggest someone break the habit of procrastination?
6. Poll your group and see how many feel they have a flat platter. How many feel their platter is tipped?
7. Discuss the flatter platter from two perspectives—the worker and the manager.

# FIVE
# UPLIFTING PRAYER

Prayer links us with the source of supernatural energy, God Himself who purifies our spirits.

With purified spirits, we remove the static and short outs on the communication line with God. Then, with the help of the Holy Spirit, we pursue progress for the Kingdom.

Praise sharpens our focus and lifts our spirits. The satisfaction that comes leads us onward. Satisfied, delighted, we want more of something so good. With new intensity we begin hungering for a holy God.

Once we are connected with the omnipotent God, our Lord Jesus gives supernatural energy to wage spiritual warfare. In His power, the "Lamb's War"[1] is winnable!


## Monday/ Purifying the Spirit

The human spirit faces a dozen corroding influences every day. The world system, the sinful nature, the satanic adversary—all work together to contaminate the human spirit.

Actual sin, of course, corrupts the human spirit, turning it away from God and all that is holy and good. More subtle are daily influences that clog the arteries of the spirit like cholesterol in the veins.

The Great Physician has an effective prescription! After citing the promises of God, the Bible explicitly tells us to purify ourselves from everything that contaminates the body and spirit. (2 Cor. 7:1).

What purifies the human spirit?

*Confession and repentance* purify the spirit. Facing up to sin and turning from it opens us up to God's cleansing grace. When we trust Christ, the atoning sacrifice of Calvary's cross cleanses us from all sin (1 John 1:9; Ps. 32:1-2; 2 Cor. 5:21).

*Restitution and reconciliation* purify the spirit. Making things right with others, including repaying money or restoring property, cleanses the spirit. Asking forgiveness, seeking to restore a shattered relationship, humbling ourselves before those who feel grieved with us—all bring a wonderful sense of relief. This step is humbling (sometimes humiliating) and never easy, but it brings inner joy.

*Bible meditation and Scripture application* purify the spirit. When the Holy Spirit speaks to us through the written Word of God, He touches the depths of our spirit. As we love, trust and obey, an inner purging takes place. *"But if we walk in the light, as he is in the light, we have fellowship with one another, and the blood of Jesus, His Son, purifies us from all sin"* (1 John 1:7).

*Worship and thanksgiving* purify the spirit. Lifting our hearts in reverence and thankfulness to the Holy One brings us into the very presence of Perfect Purity.

*Adoration and celebration* purify the spirit. Praise not only exalts God but uplifts the innermost soul as well.

Both quiet contemplation and rejoicing music have a purging quality about them.

*Prayer and petition* purify the spirit. Time spent in the presence of the living Lord always has its benefits—always. Bringing our deepest desires and specific requests to Him produces satisfaction beyond compare. The peace of God protects our hearts and minds in a marvelous way (Phil. 4:6-7).

When we unclog spiritual arteries, the grace of God freely flows through us. Guess what? We feel better, enjoy more energy and live closer to Christ. We sense His powerful presence, caring concern and energizing encouragement.

Take some time today, and every day, to purify your human spirit. Ask the Holy Spirit to guide and direct you. After all, you are His temple! (2 Cor. 7:16; Eph. 2:21-22).

---

Pray for a purified spirit.
Work on unclogging spiritual arteries.

---

## Tuesday/ Pursuing Prayer

Pursuing prayer never gives up. It dare not, it must not.

"Pursuing prayer" is another term for what Jesus called persistence, always praying and never giving up (Luke 18:1-8), asking, seeking, knocking (Matt. 7:7-8).

Pursuing prayer is already in line with God's purposes. No question exists about the Lord's will in the matter. Pursuing prayer is exclusively for fulfilling God's revealed will.

Pursuing prayer pushes Christ's purposes forward—against all obstacles, at all costs, with supernatural energy, until the goal is fulfilled.

Pursuing prayer knows what God wants and intercedes to call, equip and energize the people for it to happen. It intercedes to remove the hindrances and release the resources.

Pursuing prayer comes as a compelling concern from the Holy Spirit. The faithful servant of the Lord cannot escape it.

Pursuing prayer has its limits. One person can assume only a few major subjects for this kind of praying—or maybe only one primary concern at a time.

Pursuing prayer sets its focus on God's dream, an unmet purpose of the Lord, an unreached people group, a mission field, a movement, a church, a person, a ministry or a crying need. Whatever the focus, pursuing prayer never gives up. Never.

Pursuing prayer is the great lack among Christians today. God's purposes suffer because so few are relentlessly pursuing Him to release the power, people, resources, finances, relationships to let it happen. So few are praying against the distractions, the lethargy, the opposing forces of Satan, the wasted time, energy and money that hinder His great purposes.

Pursuing prayer always makes progress, even when it does not look like it. God honors pursuing prayer because His written Word teaches it (Eph. 6:18).

*O Father, place on my heart and the heart of many, many others one or more of your purposes for us to pursue in prayer.*

---

Pray for certainty of God's purpose.
Work at pursuing prayer.

---

## Wednesday/Pray Without Ceasing

The *King James Version* says, "Pray without ceasing." "Pray continually," says the *New International Version* of 1 Thess. 5:17.

How? How can anyone do it? It can't mean twenty-four hours a day and every minute of every hour, can it? The Christian must concentrate on work, study, people, appointments. How can anyone pray all the time? So the objections go.

A Christian can reject this command as ridiculous or impossible, and then forget it. Or he can see it as a way of life that brings power and joy.

You can choose for yourself which way to go, but as for me and my devotional life, we will pursue the path of constant communion with the living Christ.

This injunction in 1 Thess. 5:17 is not barren legalism forced to do its duty to God. No, the verse before says, *"Be joyful always"* and the verse after it says, *"Give thanks in all circumstances."* The context shows that a life of continual prayer lifts the Christian until problems become opportunities, and the bad breaks of life lead beyond disappointment to thanksgiving.

Better yet, prayer has the power to reach beyond ourselves into the lives of others and the events of our time. David Bryant reminds us that "the only thing beyond the reach of our prayers is anything outside the will of God."[2]

As we all know, prayer can penetrate barriers of personality, distance, culture or personal misunderstanding. Prayer can reach where we *cannot go* in person and can make us channels of God's blessing where we *do go*. S.D. Gordon said it well, "No matter where you are, you do more through your praying than through your personality."[3]

Let's get practical. Here are some memory-joggers that help me pray more often. Try one of these, or some other, today.

- In a committee meeting, I try to pray for whoever is talking at the moment. A neat fringe benefit is that I usually listen better.

- I sometimes pray for people in casual contacts, even strangers in cars or on the streets or in houses—especially the children. I ask the Heavenly Father to give them a good opportunity to receive Jesus Christ as Lord and Savior or to grow in Him—or simply to bless them.

- I ought to pray about the news on TV, for nations, rulers, events—and for influential personalities, sports, entertainment and politics.

- I pray for the members of my family, for pastors, staff members, missionaries and church planters.

- I often pray for the person who is talking to me.

- I sometimes pray Scripture back to God, especially passages of thanksgiving and praise.

- I try to remember to pray through my schedule for each day.

- I want to develop the habit of praying every time my watch beeps, or every time I walk through a door or sit down or stand up, or undertake any other common activity that can remind me to practice God's presence.

- I do pray in response to the Holy Spirit's nudging and urging.

Why not join me in my goal to pray more and pray better than ever before? I can think of nothing else that will so quickly and effectively make us beautiful in God's sight.

> Pray continually.
> Work at memory-joggers.

## Thursday/Silent Praise

Praise glorifies God and rejuvenates our supernatural energy.
Praise lifts our spirits,
    renews our joy,
      restores our confidence,
        brightens our day.
Praise exhilarates mind, soul and spirit.

Do you ever enjoy silent praise? Sound like a contradiction in terms? Not at all.

In silent praise the human spirit quietly lifts adoration and worship to our magnificent God—Father, Son and Holy Spirit.

One good way to begin is to read (or quote) some of the great psalms of praise. Psalms 100, 103, 145 and 146 are some of my favorites.

Then it may help to follow a praise exercise. A simple and effective one is to use the alphabet as an acrostic. With each letter think of words that praise our precious Lord and Savior.

A—amazing, awesome
B—bountiful, beautiful
C—creative, compassionate
D—(You think of the praise words.)

Sometimes silent thoughts flow in a stream of unspoken words of thanksgiving and praise. At other times no words come to mind at all, but only an inner sense of one's whole being praising the Creator, Redeemer and Coming King.

The key is focus. When total attention focuses on Jesus Christ, lifting the human spirit in adoration and worship, something marvelous happens. Out of the silence, and without articulated thoughts, we find ourselves worshiping, really worshiping, from our innermost being.

What happens next is up to God.

Sometimes He speaks out of the silence. Sometimes He grants deep peace, an inner satisfaction like no other. Sometimes He directs our thoughts to Scripture or, in His own practical way, to some matter we need to do.

Sometimes nothing "happens." We sense nothing, feel nothing, but simply know that we are silently praising the One who is worthy of our worship.

The Bible tells us to "pray in the Spirit on all occasions with all kinds of prayers and requests" (Eph. 6:18). Silent praise is one kind of prayer in the Spirit.

Silent praise. Try it. He's worth it.

---

Pray for fresh ways to praise God.
Work on varieties of silent praise.

## Friday/ Hungering and Thirsting

There is a kind of hunger that eagerly anticipates satisfaction. It is based not so much on starvation as on the memory of delight.

When I was a little boy I thought that my Grandma Hadley was the best cook in the whole world. We used to go to Grandma's house for scrumptious meals—fried chicken with mashed potatoes and gravy, corn on the cob, sweet potatoes, rolls and butter, green beans—far more delicious food than a hungry boy could ever eat. All of it was grown in her garden. She even raised the chickens!

My hunger made me look forward to Grandma's home-cooking, and I was never disappointed.

There is a thirst that eagerly anticipates satisfaction. It is based not so much on a parched tongue as on the memory of delight.

When I was a few years older, we used to go horseback riding with some family friends on the Little Camas Prairie in Idaho. There was one place in the nearby hills where we stopped at a spring to drink. That spring water was cold, pure and the most delicious I ever tasted in my whole life.

Whenever we rode in that area, I always wanted to find that same spring. My thirst made me look forward to cold, pure mountain spring water. It was wonderful.

There is a hunger and thirst for God that eagerly anticipates satisfaction. It is based not so much on spiritual starvation or dryness as on the memory of delight.

You have had the experience, and so have I, of coming into Christ's presence and finding delicious satisfaction—forgiveness, cleansing, healing, life, love, compassion, restoration. He satisfied our deepest desires with good things (Ps. 103:5).

The memory of delight keeps us coming back again and again. We enter His presence eagerly anticipating satisfaction. As Howard R. Macy writes in his excellent book, *Rhythms of the Inner Life,* "This is a thirst driven by satisfaction rather than disappointment. What we have tasted is so remarkable that we must have more and we know somehow that we can never have enough."⁴

Jesus said,

> Blessed are those who hunger and thirst for righteousness, for they will be filled (Matt. 5:6).

The psalmist wrote,

> As the deer pants for streams of water,
>   so my soul pants for you, O God.
> My soul thirsts for God, for the living God.
>   When can I go and meet with God?
>
> —Ps. 42:1-2

Revelation promises,

> For the Lamb at the center of the throne will be their shepherd; he will lead them to springs of living water.
>
> —Rev. 7:17

Let's excel in hungering and thirsting for God and for His righteousness.

Let's anticipate satisfaction as we eagerly eat the Bread of Life and drink deeply from Christ's springs of living water.

Let's find our deepest delight in God, and God alone.

Take a moment right now to recall a memory of delight when God Himself satisfied your hunger and thirst in a delicious way. Then let that memory intensify your longing to come into His presence. As you enter His holy presence, eagerly expect satisfaction.

And keep coming back again and again to enjoy Him.

> You open your hand
> and satisfy the desires of every living thing.
> —Ps. 145:16

> Pray for satisfaction.
> Work at anticipating it.

## Saturday/**Spiritual Warfare Praying**

Desire more power in prayer? It's available, readily available. Why not explore the kind of praying that the Bible describes as wrestling, struggling, standing our ground (Eph. 6:10-20; Col. 4:12)? This kind of spiritual battle is what the early Friends called the "Lamb's War."

Some people today call this type of prayer "spiritual warfare praying." Good term. Christians have always believed that the real war is spiritual rather than physical.

The people of God in all the centuries since Christ, have understood that we battle *"not against flesh and blood, but against the rulers, against the authorities, against the powers of this dark world and against the spiritual forces of evil in the heavenly realms"* (Eph. 6:12). If the terminology sounds strange, it may help to say that what the Bible is describing is nothing less than Satan and his hierarchy of demon spirits.

Allow me to share with you a spiritual warfare prayer, an edited version of the one in my book *Running the Red Lights.*[5]

*Heavenly Father, I humble myself in worship before you. To your holy name be glory, honor and praise forever! You are worthy of my adoration, devotion and thanksgiving.*

*By faith I claim the protection of the blood of the Lord Jesus Christ around and within me. In union with Christ, I take my stand against all efforts of Satan and his demons to hinder me in this time of prayer. I address myself only to the God and Father of our Lord Jesus Christ and reject any involvement of Satan in this prayer.*

(At this point, pause and rebuke Satan directly before continuing in prayer. God won't mind; He's used to interruptions. Speak these next three sentences aloud or at least let your lips move.)

Satan, I command you in the all-powerful name of the Lord Jesus Christ to leave my presence with all your demons and to go to the place where Jesus Christ sends you. I bring His blood between us and around me as a shield. In the name of the Lord Jesus Christ, I order you not to approach me in any way except by the heavenly Father's permission.

(Resume praying.)

*Righteous Father, by faith and in obedience to your command I put off the old self which is being corrupted by its deceitful desires and put on the new self, created to be like God in true righteousness and holiness. I resist all the forces of darkness that stimulate the desires of my sinful nature, and claim the appearing of the Son of God to destroy the devil's work in my life. By the power and authority of our Lord Jesus Christ, I retake any ground given to the devil and release its full control to the Holy Spirit.*

*By faith I come into union with the power, life, work and*

*ministry of the Lord Jesus Christ. I claim the power and effect of His work in Creation, Revelation in Scripture, Incarnation, Crucifixion, Burial, Resurrection, Ascension, Session (seating at the heavenly Father's right hand), Outpouring of the Holy Spirit, Intercession, Headship of the Church, rule in the Kingdom of God and Second Coming in power and great glory. I claim the power of the written and living Word of God.*

*I bring all this power to bear against Satan, his forces of evil and his strategies against me. Heavenly Father, with the divine power of weapons of righteousness that you give in Christ, I tear down Satan's strongholds in my life and in the lives of those I love. I destroy every argument and excuse for not knowing the triune God better and better. I reject the ideas and phrases that make sin attractive and plausible. By faith I claim the mind of Christ. I take every thought to make it obedient to Christ.*

*I demolish the plans of Satan formed against me today. I smash the plans of Satan against my heart, emotions, mind, will, spirit, body, soul, personality. I burst the strongholds of the enemy against any and every part of myself and bring my deepest desires to you for satisfaction.*

*In obedience to the command in your Word, I commit myself to be strong in the Lord and His mighty power. Thank you for the full armor of God that you provide. Right now I put on the belt of truth, the breastplate of righteousness, the boots of readiness that come from the gospel of peace. I hold up the shield of faith that extinguishes all the flaming arrows of the evil one. I put on the helmet of salvation. I grasp the sword of the Spirit, the Word of God. Train me to use it with supernatural ability. Stimulate me to pray on all occasions with all kinds of prayers and requests.*

*Thank you, Lord Jesus, for loving me and laying down your life for me. Open my eyes today for the opportunity to love others and to lay down my life for them. Grant me opportunities to use the spiritual gifts you have given to me in a spirit of humility, joy and service. Help me to take my focus off myself and to fix my eyes on Jesus Christ and on those whom you want me to love and serve. I enter this day with thanksgiving and praise. Open my eyes to what you are doing, holy Father, and allow me to be used of the Holy Spirit as a part of it.*

*I pray in the confidence of the wonderful name of our Lord Jesus Christ who is able to keep me from falling and present me before your presence without fault and with great joy. Amen.*

Heavy stuff? You better believe it. No one expects to go into battle with flimsy armor and light firepower. This kind of praying calls on the great truths of Scripture and Christian experience.

Don't miss this. Spiritual warfare praying has power—supernatural power. Why? Not because of human effort (although it will take all you have to persist in this kind of praying), but because it calls upon all that Christ has already done on our behalf. It brings the power of God directly against our adversary.

Spiritual warfare praying is effective for smashing the strongholds of the devil in both our own lives and the lives of those we love. I recommend that you try it daily for a minimum of thirty days—ninety is better. If it seems strange or foreign to you, consider it an adventure in improving your prayer life!

---

Pray against the adversary.
Work at spiritual warfare.

## Sunday/Discussion Questions

1. Review the list of what purifies the human spirit. In your life which ones are missing? In your church which are mentioned or practiced most often? Least often?
2. Tuesday's reading defines pursuing prayer as "a compelling concern from the Holy Spirit" that "is already in line with God's purposes." Has Christ placed a compelling concern on your heart? What is it? Do you keep praying about it?
3. Share ideas that help you pray more often and approach the goal of praying continually.
4. In your opinion is "silent praise" a contradiction of terms or another form of worship? Why not try it together as a group? Share a time when you sensed God's response.
5. Share a memory of delight when God Himself satisfied your hunger and thirst in a delicious way.
6. Search your heart before praying the spiritual warfare prayer (Saturday) and confess any sins the Holy Spirit may reveal. Then pray it daily for at least thirty days. How difficult did you find it? Did you sense any resistance from the adversary?
7. Since truth is more powerful than deceit, list some of the great Christian bulwarks of truth contained in the spiritual warfare prayer. As a group see how many Scripture passages you can locate which may be referred to in this prayer.
8. Challenge others to join you in praying the spiritual warfare prayer for thirty, sixty or ninety days.

## SIX
# EMPOWERING PEOPLE

One of the ways we tap into supernatural energy is through warm relationships with God's people.

Christian maturity and spiritual gifts come wrapped in real people. Through a vast variety of personalities God empowers us. As the Head of the Church, Christ uses each member of His Body as an energizer to others.

Think of Christians who fill the role of

exciters,
friends,
teachers,
intercessors,
peacemakers,
praisers
and many more.

The Lord knows just what we need and when. In His perfect timing He provides people in church, Christian friends or co-workers in a shared ministry who empower us. We, in turn, are used by the Holy Spirit to energize someone else just when it is needed most.

## Monday/**Exciters**

Some people are exciting. They generate enthusiasm wherever they go.

It's fun to have an exciter or two around. They make every good thing that God does seem absolutely wonderful. Exciters are motivating. They believe that what is happening is the best thing since canned pop. They convince others that now is the time to get in on the action.

Exciters, when they have up-front speaking gifts, can stir up the troops. They are great as speakers in a conference or in a motivational seminar. Everyone feels better after hearing them.

Exciters can get us through the next day or the next project. They stimulate us to believe that God has a way through the impossible—and they have seen the route. They break the impossible down to bite-size pieces and show us how it is attainable.

Exciters add a lift to our work. They make it feel so worthwhile. Exciters stretch our comfort zone until we more mundane souls will
    try something new,
      renew our efforts,
        refuse to give up,
          see a fresh possibility,
            grab hold of an idea,
              reaffirm our best work.

Exciters are not perfect people. They often attain less than they claim, but more than if they not been so excited. They often overlook some obvious flaws in what they are excited about. They sometimes have more adrenalin than good sense.

The hazards for exciters are as many as the opportunities. They can so easily become distracted from God's best. Their excitement attracts people who tempt them with money, sex or power.

Even if they miss the major snares, exciters can become sidetracked with inferior goals or objectives. Without the highest standards they can compromise with God's ideal and generate enthusiasm for what's second best.

Exciters, when they live close to God, often develop remarkable spiritual authority. Sensitive to God's Spirit and made wise by experience, exciters can become powerful leaders.

Their enthusiasm is contagious,
their communication skills grab people's attention,
their morale-building ability nourishes their
followers,
their insights empower people who work with
them.

Exciters are an essential part of God's mix in the church. Praise God for inspiring people who get us moving and keep us going.

> Pray for exciters.
> Work at generating excitement.

## Tuesday/ **Friends**

Friends—with a small *f*—are one of God's best inventions. Somehow He put within the human spirit the capacity to bond with another person in a unique way called friendship.

Friends are distinct from lovers. Romance is not part

of the mix. Friends are inclusive, not exclusive. Two friends will welcome a third, and three will welcome a fourth.

Friends are often found outside of family ties. Friendship does not always build on bloodlines or marriage connections.

Friends stand shoulder to shoulder and share a common view of their world. They share common values, insights or goals. They are intrigued by the same things.

Friends like each other. They enjoy being together. They share common experiences and conversation. They golf or fish or shop or learn or travel or play ball or worship or fellowship together. In fact, together is a big word for friends. Even when they cannot be together they would like to be.

A college friend of mine was a missionary in Bolivia for many years. He returned to the U.S.A. once every four years. We seldom wrote letters while he was out of the country, but he and his family would stop and see us on their way home. It was instant rapport. We talked like we had never been apart. The conversation picked up right where it left off, as if we were together yesterday. There's a mysterious chemistry between close friends.

Many adjectives go well with the word friend—good, close, true, lifelong, steady, valued, loyal, inseparable, beloved. These qualities describe what being a friend is all about.

Solomon, in all his wisdom writes in the Bible,

A man of many companions may come to ruin, but there is a friend who sticks closer than a brother.

—Prov. 18:24

A friend is loyal, not just standing by but sticking close. You can count on your best friends in a time of need—for help, support, encouragement and most important, just to be there.

I call my brother, Roger, a world-class friend. The quality showed up when he was still a small boy. Walking home from school, he would stop in various shops along the way and talk with the people working there. They began to look forward to his visits!

Through the years he has built deep friendships—loyal, committed, lifelong. He will do anything for his friends, and they for him. Sharing, fun, likability, conversation, social times, caring, appreciation all go into the mix.

Believe it or not, friendship is always conditional. To have a friend, you must be one. Once a friendship is cemented, it stands up against incredible adversity. "A friend loves at all times" (Prov. 17:17). However, "a gossip separates close friends" (Prov. 16:28).

The highest honor and privilege of all is to be a friend of Jesus. He said, *"You are my friends if you do what I command. I no longer call you servants, because a servant does not know his master's business. Instead, I have called you friends, for everything that I learned from my Father I have made known to you"* (John 15:14-15).

Friendship with Jesus starts with faith and obedience. It builds on communion and learning. It will reach its consummation when we see Him face-to-face and share life immortal in the age to come.

A friend—find one and be one!

---

Pray for a close friend.
Work at showing friendship.

## Wednesday/ In Praise of Sunday School Teachers

Little known, seldom praised, often overlooked, yet with incredible spiritual impact—these are Sunday School teachers. Their lasting influence on children, youth and adults can only be measured by heaven itself.

In over twenty years of ministry, I have noticed something interesting about adults who receive Christ as Lord and Savior. Almost always someone was praying for them and, as children, they went to Sunday School or a Christian camp. The seeds of the gospel planted in young hearts bore fruit in later years.

Most of us do not remember specific Sunday School lessons. Interesting, isn't it, that we *do know* what we believe, much Bible content and many Christian truths. What happened was that we internalized God's Word. The specific lessons were forgotten but the convictions remain. Thank God for Sunday School teachers and others who imprinted our lives.

Often the memory of a special Sunday School teacher remains in our mind, perhaps for a lifetime. The impression of godly character and self-giving commitment stays with a person. We may recall the respect we felt, or the closeness, or the love that this one taught us about Jesus.

When we get to heaven, and the full truth is known, my guess is that what happened through Sunday School will be far greater than we ever imagined or dreamed. How many youth were kept out of serious sin or trouble? How many adults were turned around, accepted, loved and built up in the faith? How many children were trained in the ways of Christ?

Sunday School is powerful because it communicates the truth of God's Word. And God's Word will not return empty and fruitless (Isa. 55:10-11).

It's significant that I am writing this just before summer begins. My pastor, C.W. Perry, wrote something penetrating to our whole congregation. Read carefully.

> In the summer, we have additional opportunities to win and disciple people. I really believe that Satan wants to defeat summertime ministry with the temptation for Christians to "take the summer off." I hope we all get a vacation, but God needs us to be faithful during the other eight or ten weeks during the summer. Please ask God to give *His* perspective on this near plague in most or all Christian churches today. I always hope that God doesn't take the summer off. He doesn't! Should we?

I couldn't agree more.

Praise the Lord for every faithful Sunday School teacher who faithfully teaches the Word and cares about students—even in the summertime. Your rewards will be eternal.

In the meantime, let us all take a moment to say thank you to a Sunday School teacher from the bottom of our hearts.

---

Pray for Sunday School teachers.
Work at learning or teaching God's Word.

---

### Thursday/Intercessors

Intercessors are the powerful ones.

Intercessors pray for others until God releases His grace and resources upon them.

Intercessors wage spiritual battles with the unseen forces of darkness—and win.

Intercessors sometimes rise early or stay up late or get up in the middle of the night—to pray!

Intercessors hear God's voice—not often audibly but certainly within their spirits. They often know in advance that God has answered their prayers. Everything else is just the delivery system.

And they believe! The spiritual gift of faith just might be closely linked to prayer. Intercessors claim God's promises or His inner assurances and keep praying until the answer arrives.

Intercessors have bulldog tenacity. They won't let go until what they know is God's will comes to fruition. Some have been known to pray for a certain request for years— and then God's answer arrived.

Blessed is the church that has mobilized its intercessors into a powerful army. God's presence and power will rest on that ministry.

Blessed is the person with an intercessor for a friend who calls for God's help when needed. Answers will come!

Blessed is the intercessor who develops the ministry of prayer and hones it into a fine art. What an empowering of the Body of Christ!

Intercessors know a quiet joy and peace that few others experience. They live so close to God!

Intercessors experience God's best—His presence, His power, His eternal rewards.

Intercessors touch the world. Their ministry leads to changed lives in Nepal, Angola or among the Chorti people of Guatemala.

Intercessors change world events. People in power rise or fall with their prayers. Even the demons of darkness flee in fear when an experienced intercessor invades their territory.

And when intercessors band together like a beautiful choir or a well-trained army, then watch out! What will happen next only God knows. Even human observers can see that miracles start happening in rapid-fire succession. Everything they pray for seems touched by God.

A band of committed intercessors linked to a church, a denomination, a mission organization or anything else can turn it around and bring breakthroughs otherwise impossible.

Call for intercessors, search for intercessors, motivate intercessors, pray for God to raise up more intercessors. Challenge them, motivate them, mobilize them! They are the key to releasing the Holy Spirit's power upon His people and His work.

Ask yourself, "Is God asking me to get outside of myself in prayer? Is He tugging at my heart to pray for my church, my family and relatives, my unsaved friends, my denomination, my country, my missionaries?"

If so, think about the next step. Is God expanding my horizons in prayer to other people groups, other missionaries, other ministries, other countries, other churches, other world events?

If again the answer is yes, ask one final question: Is God giving me focus in my prayers? Is He giving me something or someone specific to pray for? If so, how am I doing with the assignment?

Intercessors, arise! A dying world is waiting for

Christ's coming rescue that will result from your prayers. God seldom does anything observable apart from the prayers of His people.

> Pray for intercessors.
> Work at intercession.

## Friday/ Peacemakers

Peacemakers receive high marks from God. Jesus said in the Sermon on the Mount,

> Blessed are the peacemakers, for they will be called sons of God (Matt. 5:9).

If Jesus were preaching in one of our pulpits today, I wonder if He might say something else.

> "Blessed are the negotiators."
> "Blessed are the mediators."
> "Blessed are the reconcilers."

Peacemakers come in many forms—government negotiators, court-appointed mediators, union-management arbitrators, marriage counselors, church leaders. Some of the best peacemakers in the world are mothers.

It is not the title or the role that makes one a peacemaker, obviously, but rather the motivation and the skill.

Peacemakers quiet jangled nerves.
Peacemakers talk sense.
Peacemakers look for alternatives.
Peacemakers find common ground for
agreement.
Peacemakers appeal for change.
Peacemakers negotiate.
Peacemakers work by the rules.
Peacemakers create new rules.
Peacemakers appeal to the powerful.
Peacemakers warn the vulnerable.
Peacemakers protect the weak.

Those who work for peace, using peaceful methods, often release new energy for good into relationships (Jas. 3:18).

People in conflict feel better.
Marriages are put back together.
Working conditions improve.
Good legislation moves into operation.
Churches get outside of themselves.
Governments avoid war,
and much, much more.

Peacemakers are not spineless, wishy-washy compromisers. Often they are people with strong convictions of their own. Even Jesus Christ, the greatest reconciler of all, once said, *"Do not suppose that I have come to bring peace to the earth. I did not come to bring peace, but a sword"* (Matt. 10:34).

The context shows that He was talking about acknowledging Him before others or disowning Him; following Him in spite of family pressure or failing Him; losing one's life for His sake or grasping onto one's own life and rejecting Him. Peacemakers do not pursue peace at any price. Instead they discern ways of making peace within the limits of

> God's law,
>> cultural norms,
>>> family understandings,
>>>> shared assumptions,
>>>>> church rules,
>>>>>> company policy,
>>>>>>> government regulations,
>>>>>>>> legal precedent.

Peacemakers do incredible good, especially when they are armed with the quiet power of the Prince of Peace.

George Fox once wrote,

> The peacemaker
> hath the kingdom
> and is in it;
> and hath dominion
> over the peace-breaker
> to calm him
> in the power of
> God.
> —from an epistle of 1652

*"Turn from evil and do good; seek peace and pursue it"* (Ps. 34:14).

---

Pray for peace.
Work as a peacemaker.

## Saturday/ **Praisers**

Praisers are people who see the best in everything—and say so.

They are fun to be near—positive, upbeat, appreciative, enthusiastic.

Far from a Pollyanna blindness, praisers are often intensely critical of the few things they do not like. Please note that they criticize things—systems, procedures, ideas, wrong beliefs—but seldom people. Praisers see the best in people.

After you have given anything your best shot, a praiser will give you credit—usually in the presence of others.

After a musical special, sermon, Sunday School class or all-church event you can see the praiser smiling and saying,

"Wasn't that marvelous!"

"Wonderful!"

"God really spoke to me through that."

"We have the best _____ of any church around!"

Praisers are not phony, not gushers, not putting on a front. They see the best and point it out to others with genuine appreciation.

Praise God for praisers. They love the Lord and the Lord's people with a passion. They have tapped into His joy and enthusiasm. They enjoy the best of everything around them.

Praisers keep the rest of us going. Receiving praise in humbleness is accepting refreshment from the Lord. It adds joy, motivation, self-worth and dignity to our lives.

Praisers always have friends and acquaintances in abundance. No mystery. All but the critical enjoy their presence.

Praisers most often are faithful in their own lives and

ministries. One reason they so often see the best in others is because they are present to notice. When the best sermon, best lesson, best solo, best Bible study, best act of compassion is given—*they are there!*

Think of a couple of praisers by name. Thank God for them. Then drop them a note or tell them in person how much they mean to you and others.

One more thing: Believe them. When they praise you they are telling the truth from their perspective. Receive it as God's gift!

---

Pray for praisers.
Work at giving praise.

---

## Sunday/ Discussion Questions

1. Name some exciters you know. What makes them so excited about God's work?
2. Who is your best friend or closest group of friends? What does it take to build lasting friendships?
3. Name a Sunday School teacher or two who made a lasting contribution to your life.
4. Do you know any intercessors? Name them. In your church are intercessors organized to pray together? Is God asking you to get outside of yourself in prayer?
5. Why do peacemakers sometimes have a bad name? Who are the most effective peacemakers that you know? What methods do they use to make peace?

6. Name some praisers you know. Do they make you and others feel good? Are they genuine? Do we need more praisers? How often do you give others honest praise?
7. What other kinds of empowering people do you know? Name some and explain how they energize God's people.

## SEVEN
# PRESSURIZED ENERGY

When under intense pressure we need supernatural energy the most.

Some pressures are beyond our control. Culture rot, tough times, trials and troubles, conflict and divisions, suspicion and betrayal all take their toll on our energy level. The good news is that supernatural energy works best when the heat is on, when we find ourselves in the boiling cauldron of life and feel like we are going to explode.

### Monday/**Culture Rot**

Back in the 1940s D. Elton Trueblood declared that ours was a "cut-flower society."[1] The Western world was severed from its Christian roots and doomed to decay. How prophetic!

Over forty years later shattered families, rising divorce rates, drug and alcohol addiction, filthy pornography, AIDS and other sexually transmitted diseases, eating disorders, child abuse, overcrowded prisons—all witness to the truth of his prediction.

What we see today is culture rot—and the ongoing decay is invading our thinking, our homes, our schools and, let us say it with tears, even our churches.

Let us warn one another about the dangers of culture rot.

*Ravenous consumerism.* Money and what it will buy has become a god in our society. Prestige is measured by affluence rather than by integrity and character. Watch out for its rotting counterparts:

- Consumer Christianity—looking for what I can get instead of what I can give.
- Tipping God—accumulating wealth for retirement instead of giving tithes, offerings and Faith Promises.
- Weekending—justifying Sunday youth sports and family activities instead of an every week commitment to worship and Sunday School.

*Skeptical secularism.* Secular humanism builds a way of life that leaves God out. While Christians resist, they still fall prey to the secular mindset that leaves little room for God's direct intervention in our lives. Watch out for:

- Last-ditch healing—praying for miraculous healing only after all medical hope is gone instead of turning to Christ first.
- Silent skepticism—chalking up answers to prayer to mere coincidence instead of discerning God's mighty work.
- Spiritual amnesia—forgetting the great things Christ has done in our lives instead of overflowing with thankfulness.

*Self-indulgent individualism.* The spirit of our age has turned personal freedom into self-indulgence. Chuck Colson likens this radical individualism to a new barbarian invasion.[2] The new barbarians are destroying homes, schools, political institutions and leaving moral virtues dead or wounded.

The church is especially susceptible to this kind of culture rot:

- Entertainment mentality—complaining about "not getting fed" when the preaching and teaching are not humorous or colorful enough instead of fervently praying for and constantly encouraging the pastor and teachers.
- Me first—excusing sin with trite phrases that are found nowhere in the Bible such as "God wants me to be happy" instead of pursuing holiness out of reverence for God.
- Easy forgiveness—looking for God to forgive known sin without real repentance, instead of seeking a Christ-given change in thinking and personal behavior.
- Immorality overload—considering lewd language, swearing, sexual immorality and vulgar violence in movies, videos and music as normal and harmless, instead of finding forms of recreation and entertainment that please our Savior.

It's time for all of us to agree with the man who wrote, "You don't have to climb into the trash can to smell the garbage."

All it takes for culture rot to spread is for good people to do nothing. Yet we need wisdom. We can remind ourselves of Jesus' parables of the wheat and the weeds

(Matt. 13:24-30). We can grow as good grain without trying to weed out of our fellowship everyone who disagrees
with our own viewpoint.

Culture rot need not destroy us. We can push our roots
deep into the Lord Jesus Christ and tap into the Source of
supernatural energy and power. We can ask the divine
Gardener to prune every branch of our lives that bears no
fruit (John 15). When our connection with the True Vine is
healthy and fruitful, culture rot around us becomes fertile
soil for the transforming gospel of Christ.

Culture rot or fertile soil—which way will our decaying
society affect you and me?

---

> Pray against culture rot.
> Work at planting seeds in fertile soil.

---

## Tuesday/Traction out of Trouble

Every miracle in the Bible began with a human problem.

Every dramatic answer to prayer came in a time of
trouble—
    the Exodus from Egypt,
      the crossing of the Red Sea,
        the leveling of Jericho's walls.

Recall Gideon with his lamps and trumpets before the
Midianites,
    David with his sling before Goliath,
      Elijah with his prayer of faith before the prophets
of Baal.

Let your mind race to prophets and apostles and Jesus
Himself.

Before each dramatic act of God there was a crying need for help. Every crisis gives God a fresh opportunity. He wants to use evil for good, teach us to trust and obey Him and build strong character through fiery trial.

Do not be misled. Evil is still awful; wrong is yet sinful. Pain hurts and suffering brings real agony. In no way do Christians escape pressures and frustration in this world.

Paul once wrote an astonishing thing about trouble: *"We also rejoice in our sufferings"* (Rom. 5:3). The famous apostle was teaching that a Christian can smile through the tears. And he knew why.

As a master sculptor, God uses suffering to shape character. The hammer and chisel in the Lord's skillful hands are pain and trouble. The Christian learns to count it pure joy when the Lord's hammer blows hit hard and the constant chipping of His chisel cuts deep.

With superb craftsmanship the Lord is forming something beautiful, something good. God does not hurry. He knows precisely how much time it takes to develop the best character qualities.

Other inspired writers of the Bible with one voice affirm that the Christian can expect suffering as part of God's plan. *"Many are the afflictions of the righteous,"* observed David (Ps. 34:19, *NASB*). *"In this world you will have trouble,"* Jesus predicted (John 16:33). James assumes his readers will *"face trials of many kinds"* (Jas. 1:2).

A heart set free from inner turmoil never depends on serene circumstances on the outside—never, never, never.

Every trial leads to a decision. The tough times force a choice to become a better person or a worse one. Character either matures or crumbles depending on the response to God while the pressure is on.

A bedrock principle in the Bible is that God uses evil, which is really evil, to produce something good (Gen. 50:20). The informed Christian knows God's promise that in everything, no matter how tragic it appears, God is working for the good of those who love Him (Rom. 8:28).

From a human point of view, some suffering appears so senseless that only eternity will reveal the secret hand of God at work. Even the thought of the ten thousand hungry people who die each day because of malnutrition and related diseases brings a lump to my throat.

Or think about the Holocaust under the Nazi regime. The sinfulness and cruelty of human being against human being is almost beyond belief. Even in the midst of such terrible tragedies come heroic stories of faith and perseverance. While in a Nazi prison camp Corrie ten Boom inspired a whole generation with her dying sister Betsy's insight that "there is no pit so deep that God is not deeper still."

Joni Eareckson Tada has turned paralysis into a powerful testimony of God's faithfulness in suffering. She sings, speaks, paints with a brush in her teeth and has started an organization called Joni and Friends to encourage other disabled people.

God can give you traction out of trouble. Pursue Him, trust Him, obey Him, give Him time to work—and see what happens.

In the long run you will see Christ at work.

---

Pray for relief from suffering.
Work at smiling through the tears.

## Wednesday/ Trouble at the Top

Church splits seldom start at the fringes.

Outsiders or newcomers cannot divide a fellowship. When the adversary wants to ruin a ministry he most often starts from within.

In his cunning deceit, the evil one may drive a wedge between the leaders and the followers. When they disagree, one or the other simply leaves. The church is hurt, but it does not split.

To split a church, the Prince of Darkness gets the top leaders, paid or unpaid, into conflict. The issues themselves may be matters of philosophy or policy or even doctrine. Beneath the issues often lie power struggles and personality clashes.

When leaders fail to work out their differences, they soon rally two different groups of followers to choose up sides. The stage is set for a split.

What is the solution?

It's often found by obeying the first commandment of loving God and in keeping the second most important commandment: *"Love your neighbor as yourself"* (Matt. 22:39) and the new commandment that Jesus gave, *"Love one another. As I have loved you, so you must love one another"* (John 13:34).

I am indebted to Rich Buhler, host of Los Angeles radio KBRT's "Talk from the Heart," for a helpful insight.[3] He points out that many Christians in family conflict, or any other kind, confuse love and approval.

Love is unconditional and cannot be earned. It relates to being—who a person is. We owe all people love, even if we disapprove of their actions.

Approval is conditional and must be earned. It relates

to doing—how a person acts. We approve or disapprove of what people do.

The most common mistake is to withhold love when we feel disapproval. People stop speaking or start backbiting or begin politicking. Or they run, fight, blame or quit.

When leaders strongly disagree, they claim to love each other but their actions do not show it. They are withholding love, violating Jesus' commandment, living in sin.

What is needed instead is effective disapproval. This is most often done verbally, person-to-person, eyeball-to-eyeball, beginning in private. Matt. 18:15-17 gives the sequence for trying to resolve conflict by effectively expressing disapproval. Other ways, Rich Buhler suggests, of expressing disapproval include writing a letter, arranging a special event to discuss the problem, sharing specific facts along with inner feelings and suggesting workable solutions.[4]

Prevention is better than cure. It is far better to forgive one another and bear with one another in love than to allow a rift that leads to open conflict.

When conflict does come, and it surely will, then we need to resolve it quickly and biblically. This includes expressing disapproval while continuing to give loads of unconditional love with a right motive.

No better example of this can be found in the Bible than Jesus' dealing with Judas Iscariot. Here is a model of dealing with trouble at the top. Jesus shows us that in some cases there are no easy solutions. Even with supernatural energy it may cost a crucifixion to deal with deep conflict Jesus' way.

Are we willing to pay the price to resolve trouble at the top? Do we have the courage to express verbal disapproval while giving lots of love?

Remember, in God's plan, after a crucifixion comes a resurrection.

---

Pray for unconditional love.
Work at distinguishing love and approval.

---

## Thursday/Settling Conflict

When you stop to think about it, there are only three ways to settle conflict.
Reconciliation
Arbitration
Separation
*Reconciliation is God's plan* (Eph. 2:14-16; Matt. 5:23-24). Our Lord's choice is for us to claim the peace of Christ and make every effort to win our brother over (Matt. 18:15).
*Arbitration is man's plan* (Matt. 18:16; Acts 15:1-35). When no reconciliation takes place, the Bible calls for Christian leaders to try to mediate or arbitrate. They listen to both sides, offer sound counsel and try to work out an acceptable solution.
*Separation is Satan's plan* The Bible implores us to strive for unity (Eph. 4:3; Rom. 15:5). The adversary tries to disrupt this unity whenever he can.
The only time the Bible calls for separation is when believers and unbelievers are yoked together (2 Cor. 6:14-18). Those who openly deny the faith and oppose the teaching of sound doctrines of Scripture receive scathing

denunciations in the New Testament (Jude 3-19; 2 Pet. 2). Even then it makes sense to attempt corrective church discipline before separation takes place.

In our human experience, broken as it is, times come when all attempts at reconciliation and arbitration fail. Separation takes place, like it or not. More often than not this separation comes not from doctrinal issues, but rather from power struggles and personality conflicts. Jesus had His Judas Iscariot who betrayed Him. The one thing worse than separation is a dirty separation.

Sometimes Christian leaders separate simply because they cannot agree. After the wonderful account of reconciliation of the church in Acts 15:35, the rest of the chapter briefly reports the separation of Paul and Barnabas over a personnel issue concerning John Mark. Even after separation a healing of spirit and oneness in the faith can come. Paul's later writings in the New Testament show both respect for Barnabas and reconciliation with John Mark.

So often when separation takes place both sides feel like victims. And in reality most conflicts are indeed two-sided.

The only answer is to fight with spiritual weapons. Love our enemies, do good to those who hate us, bless those who curse us, pray for those who mistreat us—just as our Lord Jesus taught us (Matt. 5:43-45; Luke 6:27-36).

My heart goes out to the innocent who are caught in the middle—children in a divorce, the undecided in a church split, employers and employees caught in an unwanted management-union conflict. For the victims an old saying comes to mind. "Seek God's peace first, then His direction." A monumental challenge is to live in Christ's energizing peace when others disappoint or betray us.

This brings us full cycle to making every attempt to bring about reconciliation again. Reconciliation, after all, is still God's plan.

> Pray for reconciliation.
> Work at arbitration.

### Friday/ Watching the Yellow Lights

A strong marriage enhances a good ministry. Lose your marriage and you lose your ministry.

Psychologist James Dobson once said in talking about adultery, "In any group of one hundred people there is a secret." Most counselors will agree.

Christians *do* fall into affairs, and "fall" is the right word, because the strange truth is that most of them were never looking for adultery.

An adulterous affair does not "just happen." The relationship goes through predictable stages. Think of these stages as warnings, as flashing yellow lights to alert the unwary:

*Beware of emotional delight outside of marriage that is not taking place within it.* An emotional affair precedes a physical one. During this "conversation stage" everything seems innocent and fun until the friendship begins to seem more fulfilling than your own marriage.

*Double-check your feelings if you find yourself looking forward to the next hug.* The second step toward adultery comes in the "touching stage." There is a time to hug and a time not to hug. Some hugging simply communicates healthy friendship and Christian caring. However, when the person is the same one who gives emotional delight in the conversation stage, watch out. The electricity of subtle sensuality flows easily through touch. Romance and arousal respond to comfort and inner delight.

*Watch out for friendships that become too close.* The third step toward an adulterous affair is a male-female friendship that enters the "possession stage." With tender talk, emotional delight, warm hugs and romantic signals, a couple begins to believe they belong to each other. Gifts, phone calls, notes, lunch, dinner—all communicate that this relationship has turned possessive. The couple resort to excuse-making and lying to their spouses to cover their hidden times together. Yet because they are not sleeping together, they convince themselves it is not adultery.

Can we affair-proof our marriages? Only as we stand in joyful obedience to God, balancing grace and discipline in our lives, will we build fidelity and satisfaction.

More than ever, marriages are strained by time pressures. We put our energies into our jobs, our children and other outside commitments, including Christian service. Too often we come home drained and fatigued, with nothing left for our spouses. While relentless time pressures yield no easy answers, a few tips may help keep a marriage romantic and fulfilling:

- Talk to your husband or wife by phone at least once a day. Keep it tender.
- Take a moment to write a loving note.
- Buy a card or a little gift, one with personal meaning. Make it humorous or romantic.
- Eat a meal out together at least once a week. If you cannot afford the meal, buy a Coke or take a walk together. Find time to talk and share your feelings.

- In a crowd, catch your mate's eye from a distance and smile.
- Tell your spouse's mother or best friend what you appreciate most about your mate. (It will get back.)
- Pray together daily—every other day if you are simply too exhausted.

In a hundred ways keep the love overflowing. A warm marriage is always better than a shady affair.

---

Pray for a warm marriage.
Work at watching the yellow lights.

---

### Saturday/Holy Ground and Battle Ground

I love holy ground experiences—those dramatic, life-changing times when God moves in.

These are the highlight experiences of life with the Lord. I think of when I first received Christ, felt the infilling of the Holy Spirit, sensed a call to serve Him, discovered my spiritual gifts. Pause and think of those times when you encountered God in a life-changing, overwhelming way.

It may have been a rush of emotion or a time of fresh insight or a deep sense of inner peace. It may have been a moment of repentance or faith or joy. Certainly it was accompanied by a deep assurance of God's presence.

A wooden altar at the front of a small church,
    a musical concert with a black singer,

a routine Wednesday night prayer meeting,
a youth conference sparkling with fervor,
a fully relaxed vacation in the beauty of
creation,
a fund-raising banquet with our pastor
speaking,
a walk alone as dawn was breaking,
each of these became for me a setting for a holy ground
experience.

Christ spoke; I responded. He moved in; I was
changed. He revealed something of Himself or His plan;
my life was altered. Always, always these times produced
long-lasting benefits. *"For the Lord is good and his love
endures forever"* (Ps. 100:5).

Contrast these holy ground experiences with battleground struggles.

On battleground God seems distant, if present at all.
The struggle—temptation, trial, hardship, burden or ach-
ing emptiness—takes all the energy I can muster, and
more.

The problem does not go away. At times it only seems
to get worse. I feel—and surely you have, too—trapped,
pressured, oppressed, harassed, miserable, helpless,
hopeless. Supernatural energy brings no solution.

Sometimes there is no way out, no escape from battleground struggles. After battling, praying, crying, seeking
help, trying to believe, fasting, regrouping, forgiving,
hurting—the only answers I hear are, "hang in there,"
"put up with it," "stick it out," "don't give up," "back off
and be quiet." So little comfort.

In holy ground experiences, God does it all. We simply
respond—love, trust, obey, enjoy. In battleground struggles it feels like we do it all
—cope, hurt, survive.

Every Christian I know has spent some time on holy ground and some on battleground.

Why? Why does God leave for each of us at least one area of life that is a constant struggle?

A satisfying answer comes from those who have walked the longest with the Lord—and won on battleground.

> Only here do we learn the greatest lessons of faith.
> Only here do we get an honest look at our worst side—and our need to change.
> Only here do we prove the grace of God when it doesn't feel good.
> Only here do we understand deeply the hurt of fellow strugglers.
> Only here do we fully grasp the pain of the cross, the power of the Resurrection and the promise of Christ's return.

The strange truth is that often the hardest times in life, in retrospect, turned out to be some of the best times. Not the pain, but the progress made it worth the battle.

And what about the other times? What about the evil that always seemed intensely wrong and without redeeming value?

I don't have all the answers. But I am looking forward to asking the One who does when I meet Him face-to-face. Are you?

---

Pray to trust Christ on holy ground.
Work to obey Him on battleground.

## Sunday/ Discussion Questions

1. What signs of culture rot do you see in society? In the Church? How can culture rot be seen as fertile soil for the gospel?
2. Share a time when God gave you traction out of trouble. How can a person learn to smile through the tears?
3. How is it possible to show love and express disapproval at the same time? Under what conditions does disapproval change our actions?
4. What are some practical steps toward reconciliation with a "Judas Iscariot?" Why do we so often bypass Christian arbitration or mediation?
5. Does any condition or circumstance ever justify adultery? What can be done to "affair-proof" a marriage?
6. Share some holy ground experiences that have been deeply meaningful.
7. Share a battleground struggle and how you overcame it with God's help? What benefits came to you as a result?

EIGHT

# CHRIST CONNECTION

Christ has so much to receive, if only we will share it. He has such wonderful changes to make within us, if only we will allow it. He has so much of Himself to share, if only we will respond rightly.

He is worthy of our best and capable of dealing with our worst. He invites us to come into living union with His power, life, work, ministry and person. He wants to rescue us from starvation and lavish us with love.

For supernatural energy to flow, connect with Christ, its source.

## Monday/**God's Picnic**

Ever been late in getting ready for a church picnic? And a little short on cash? I have.

Since my wife was out of town, I thought about going by Colonel Sander's Kentucky Fried Chicken for some fast food to take out. On second thought, considering the cash crunch and how late it was, I just raided the refrigerator for something quick and easy.

A crummy old sandwich slapped together quick, an

apple and a couple of the kids' school-lunch snack items stuffed in a brown paper sack, and I was on my way to the park.

I don't remember everything the other family spread out on the long picnic table we shared, but I do remember the chicken—and that they had plenty of food.

There I sat with my embarrassing brown-bag sandwich next to a gracious family who laid out a tablecloth on the rough table and filled it with a feast fit for a king.

"Why don't you join us?" they asked. "We have more than enough. We can share."

"Oh, no. That's okay. I'm fine." I mumbled some excuses with my eye on the delicious chicken.

"Come on. We can all eat together. Pass Chuck the chicken."

And so we shared. My brown bag wasn't much but they didn't seem to mind. The fried chicken and potato salad and potato chips and chocolate cake tasted delicious. They enjoyed giving and, before long, I forgot about myself and joined in the fun. We had a wonderful time together.

When I stop to think about it, isn't that the way it is at God's picnic? I show up late with a brown bag of leftover energy. It isn't much and I feel slightly embarrassed to even share His picnic table.

With warmth and laughter He says, "Let's share." Without a moment of hesitation He spreads out a feast of energizing spiritual food that looks good and tastes even better.

He takes what little I brought and mixes it with His table of delights before saying, "Pass Chuck the chicken." I can hardly believe it. I am eating at the King's table.

When I think of it this way, it's amusing and pitiful to watch some people at the picnic who clutch their brown bags and refuse to share. "This sandwich is mine! God's not getting everything I've got. If you don't look out for yourself, nobody else will."

So they eat their stale sandwiches and paltry leftovers and complain about the food. Half-starved, they never have enough energy to enjoy the rest of the picnic.

Living for yourself is a sure way to miss God's feast. Forget about yourself. The Lord doesn't need your brown bag, but you need His chicken. God isn't trying to sap your already depleted energy. He wants to share His resurrection power with you.

The resurrected Jesus provides supernatural energy for your struggles. He takes what little you've got and mixes it with His bounteous provisions.

Enjoy the feast![1]

---

> Pray for God's feast.
> Work at sharing the food.

---

## Tuesday/ Your Hidden Life

Everyone has a hidden life, an inner world that few others see.

Everyone has a hidden life of private thoughts. Personal thoughts "comment" on self, people, events, ideas and God Himself.

Everyone has a hidden life of driving motives. Some are good and right, others can be wrong and sinful.

Everyone has a hidden life of moral decisions. Morality or immorality does not just happen; it comes from the heart.

Everyone has a hidden life of unseen admirations. People, goals, ideas are admired, cherished, desired, pursued.

Everyone has a hidden life of personal values—what's held as precious or what is treated as garbage, what's important or what's a waste, what's worth giving time to or what there's never enough time for.

What's scary is that something within the hidden life is corrupt, diseased, distorted. It's not all good; part of the inner life is desperately evil.

It brings up terrible thoughts.

It drives a person with selfish motives.

It makes immoral decisions.

It admires bad people, wrong goals and stupid ideas.

It resists the highest and best values and welcomes the lowest and worst.

The Bible calls this bent toward evil the old self, the sinful nature, the flesh, the uncircumcised heart.

For those who come to Jesus Christ in repentance and faith, the good news is that He is the Great Physician. He operates on the old, sinful nature when we trust Him as Savior and Lord.

Visualize a divine operating room. The Supreme Surgeon has scrubbed and put on his surgery gown, sterile gloves and mask. The one on the operating table is you.

It's open heart surgery—not physical but rather on the hidden life of the heart. The Great Physician works confidently. With scalpel in hand He circumcises the heart.

Part of the surgical procedure is repair and replacement. Private thoughts are redirected, driving motives rechanneled, immoral decisions reversed, unseen admirations refocused, personal values reformed.

The Great Physician never does the surgery of spiritual circumcision (Col. 2:11) in order to make things worse. He never takes anything out of the hidden, inner life without putting something better in its place.

The fullness of God, the new self, the Spirit of life are all carefully stitched in with skill and precision.

After surgery Christ the Divine Doctor prescribes therapy and medication. The therapy is to push and pull. Push off the old self with its practices and pull on the new (Col. 3:5-11). For heart medicine, the Doctor prescribes seven pills to be taken daily.

1. Meditation on Christ (Col. 3:1-2)
2. Peace (Col. 3:15)
3. Prayer (Phil. 4:6-7)
4. Thanksgiving (Col. 3:15)
5. God's Word (Col. 3:16)
6. Christian music (Col. 3:16)
7. Renewed purpose (Col. 3:17)

The hidden life of the heart is repaired. The recovery period after surgery is short and pleasant. The therapy and medication, however, must be taken for the rest of our lives.

The result is so refreshing and energizing. The hidden life of thoughts, motives, decisions, admiration and values are freed from disease and distortion and made healthy and whole.

Do you need to make an appointment with the Great Physician?

---

Pray for heart circumsion.
Work at spiritual therapy and medication.

## Wednesday/The Love and Fear of God

"Oh, love of God, how rich and pure! How measureless and strong!"[2] we sing in the great hymn. God's love, and our love for Him in return, motivates service and devotion as nothing else can.

When the Bible speaks of the "fear of the Lord," however, some people feel uncomfortable, or even confused. How can a Christian fear the God of love—or love a God who expects us to fear Him?

It helps me when I grasp the truth that true love of God and the holy fear He deserves never contradict each other. True worship includes both, like catching two reflections of light from one perfect diamond. Experiencing God in His infinite power and tender mercy evokes both awesome fear and unselfish love.

The one who fears God best loves Him most.

Loving God without any fear turns a Christian's faith soft, wishy-washy, sentimental. Fearing God without genuine love, on the other hand, produces a belief that is hard, cold and brittle. Mix the two, without any impurities, and what emerges is courageous devotion.

Those who love Christ and fear God under the inspiration of the Holy Spirit seldom lack for courage when their faith is challenged, opposed or ridiculed.

On a human level most people mix a measure of love and fear in the best of relationships. We fear anything that will damage one we love or that will hinder our closeness to that special person. We teach our children healthy fears.

*"Stop, look and listen before you cross the street."*

*"Don't touch that hot stove."*

We train our youth to fear damaging a good friendship by abusing it in any way. Likewise the fear of God keeps us from doing things that damage our relationship with Him or harm others.

The fear of the Lord, of course, goes far beyond any human analogy. When we experience Him in power and majesty, we may find ourselves on our knees awestruck, trembling in adoration, quaking in holy fear. It was this kind of worship that first gave Friends the nickname of Quakers.

Let's love Christ, and fear Him, with eyes wide open to who He really is and hearts aflame with a desire to please Him!

---

Pray to experience God more fully.
Work at awesome fear and unselfish love.

---

### Thursday/ Worthy of Our Unworthiness

The Lamb that was slain, our crucified and resurrected Lord is worthy. He is worthy of honor, glory and praise. He is worthy of the best we have to give—our strengths, riches, achievements, everything.

Not only is He worthy of our best, He is also worthy of our worst.

Many organizations, companies, governments and churches are more than happy to receive our best. They gladly take any contributions or praise that we will bring. Precious few want our worst, unless there is a price tag attached.

Our Lord Jesus Christ died and rose again in order to deal with our worst—our sins, rebellion, apathy, self-centeredness. He takes our worst and exchanges it for His best. Good deal!

When we fall short, when we disappoint ourselves and others, when we fail, He is worthy to deal with both our actions and the consequences. He is worthy because He has total love and unlimited power. He not only accepts us, He also changes us.

In a similar way, He is worthy of receiving our uneasy sense of unworthiness. He relieves our inadequacies, fears and failures.

Some of us do not share our unworthiness with others easily. Only the closest family members and friends hear from our lips about our unworthy feelings. It takes courage to share shame and self-blame with a friend.

Yet we can bring all our hidden feelings of unworthiness, all our shortcomings, all our faults to the Lord Jesus with complete confidence. He is able and worthy of dealing with our dark side. He can handle damaged emotions, painful memories, shattered expectations and broken dreams.

He is worthy. In fact, He is the only one qualified to give deep inner healing and lasting relief.

We will never become deserving. We will never qualify as those to whom God owes a debt. In one sense we will always remain unworthy of His grace and glory. Yet part of His miraculous work is to take our sense of unworthiness, transform us and give us genuine worth.

> He created us in His own image. That gives us worth.
> He died and rose to redeem us. That gives us worth.
> He transforms us into the very image of Christ. That gives us worth.

While we remain undeserving, He gives us worth and that makes us truly worthy. Who else qualifies as deserving of our worst and our best, our unworthiness and our worth?

*"Worthy is the Lamb, who was slain, to receive power and wealth and wisdom and strength and honor and glory and praise!"* (Rev. 5:12).

---

> Pray to receive worthiness.
> Work to release unworthiness.

---

## Friday/ Railroad Tracks

Christ is like eternal railroad tracks with no beginning and no end.

My good friend, Toni Baldwin, once shared this analogy with me. Each of our lives is like a train car on its own railroad tracks. We have a definite point of beginning and, for this life, a definite point of ending.

In His sovereign will our heavenly Father arranges for our tracks and Christ's to intersect at certain points in our lives. In those moments we have the opportunity to switch over to Christ's tracks.

On His tracks we begin to live "in Christ," the phrase used so often by the apostle Paul. In Christ (on His tracks) we have eternal life now and in heaven.

In Christ we experience forgiveness, cleansing, hope. As we stay on His tracks, we enjoy all the benefits of Christ's life, work, person and ministry. On Christ's tracks we experience the creativity in our lives that comes from His work as Creator.

In Christ we learn and trust God's revelation in Scripture. Because it's personal and real, God's Word comes alive for us.

In Christ, pulled by His powerful locomotive on His tracks, we become fully human, fully a man or fully a woman. Just as the Lord descended to become fully man, so we ascend to a new humanity in Him.

On Christ's tracks we benefit by all the atoning power of the cross. We stand acquitted, redeemed, reconciled because our Lord Jesus turned aside God's wrath as He took our place in becoming sin for us.

In Christ we die to sin and identify with His burial. In union with Him we will one day conquer death and escape hell.

On Christ's tracks we share His resurrection. We rise to newness of life and living hope. On the Day of the Lord we too will rise from the dead with a resurrection body.

In Christ we ascend to the right hand of the Father and are seated with Him in His place of authority. All evil powers are under His feet and—surprise—under ours.

On Christ's tracks we know what it is to wait. Our lives are hidden with Christ in God until the time when He is revealed for all the world to see.

In Christ we benefit by His intercession. Christ cares for those on His train and He prays with great effect for them. We benefit more than we will ever know in this life.

On Christ's tracks we experience the outpouring of the Holy Spirit. He empowers His train, His church. He teaches, counsels, purifies, motivates, gifts, works, becomes fruitful and so much more.

In Christ we connect to the Head of the Church. All the roles of Head of His Body, bridegroom of His Bride, architect and builder of His Building, author and finisher of His Book, *The Faith*, all are fulfilled in our lives. We fellowship, worship and witness with others on Christ's train.

On Christ's tracks we receive power from His rule in the kingdom of God and His reign in the universe.

In Christ we look ahead and see down the tracks what is coming. We anticipate with eagerness His Second Coming in power and great glory. We will stand before the judgment seat of Christ, avoid hell and gain heaven.

On Christ's tracks we now experience the energy of the written and living Word of God.

There's more. So much more. But we will never experience it until our railroad car switches onto Christ's tracks.

Stay on track.

> Pray to switch onto Christ's tracks.
> Work to stay on track.

## Saturday/ **Rescue Plus**

While President Richard M. Nixon was in the White House, he rented a small home to East Whittier (CA) Friends Church. His mother used to live there, a godly woman who loved the Lord Jesus Christ and was faithful in our church. The President, in honor of his mother who had gone to be with the Lord some years before, charged the church only $50 per month for the house.

At that time I was going to Fuller Theological Seminary and was on the staff of East Whittier Friends Church. They graciously allowed us to live in the Nixon house. That privilege, which became somewhat dubious during

Watergate days, even led to my wife, Nancy, and I being interviewed on the evening news of NBC, CBS and ABC television. It seems that the President had claimed quite a bit of money in improvements and repairs that the media questioned!

Behind the Nixon house was an open field in which the weeds grew high until the mowers came through. After one of those mowings our young children, Kirk and Lisa, who were then preschool age, found a mother cat that had been killed. Evidently she had not escaped the mower blades.

A few weeks earlier this stray cat had kittens in the field, and one little black and white one was missed by the vicious blades of the mower. Our kids found the orphan, and they just *had* to have it. So home it came to our Nixon house.

This fearful little kitten arched its back, hissed and bit at us. In all his insecurity, he was not at all appreciative of his new owners. He did not seem to catch on to the truth that our rescue had saved him from almost certain death.

We named the black and white orphan "Boots" and took him in with love and cat food! He became our pet and, in time, his attitude changed. Before many months passed, I would often feel Boots rubbing against my leg, purring and arching his back for a caress.

Was this the same cat that hissed and scratched and bit? What made the difference? As I think about it, the difference was "rescue plus."

We might have put out a little food and water and then ignored him. He would have scavenged for himself, and I doubt he would have purred and rubbed our legs and looked for a loving caress.

Instead we took him in, lavished him with love, and he turned into an affectionate pet. I wonder if it is not much the same with new people who come to our churches. We can allow them to find their basic spiritual food and scratch for themselves, while we keep busy with our own friends and acquaintances. Or we can go out of our way to make a new friend, show some interest and build a redemptive relationship.

What can motivate me to take the time and make the extra effort to show love to a spiritually hungry stranger? Maybe it would help if I looked again at the "rescue plus" policy of Jesus—sure rescue plus lavish love.

One day Jesus reached out His hand to rescue my life and I noticed the scratch marks on His hand—that I had made!

> Pray for Jesus' rescue.
> Work at giving lavish love.

## Sunday/ **Discussion Questions**

1. Share a time when someone's generous sharing lifted your spirits. Did it feel like a picnic? A feast? A delicious meal for someone dying of hunger?
2. Discuss our hidden lives—thoughts, motives, decisions, admirations, values. Are they really hidden? To what extent do they show?
3. Is Christ's surgery of circumcising the heart instantaneous or a long process. What other kinds of spiritual therapy and medication does the Bible suggest?
4. Is the fear of God ever unhealthy? What distorted

images do we have of Him? In your opinion, why do so many people today fear Satanism yet have no fear of disobeying God?

5. What does the author mean by "worthy of our unworthiness?" Do we accept other people the way that He accepts us? How can we give a sense of self-worth and dignity to others?

6. How do we switch onto Christ's tracks? Share some practical applications of living "in Christ."

7. Share how the "rescue plus" policy of Jesus changed your life. What can we do to get outside of ourselves in reaching out to newcomers in our churches?

NINE

# SPIRIT POWER

The Holy Spirit is the Supernatural Energizer.

He works within us in a variety of special ways—good impulses, crucial longings, fullness of faith and power, spiritual gifts and Christlike character, to name a few.

A few insights into His working may heighten our awareness of His energy. As we respond to Him in faith and obedience, good things begin to happen within us and through us.

## Monday/**Good Impulses**

Competence means living in an organized, efficient, time-saving, tightly-scheduled world. Time pressure and work load are twin weights resting on broad shoulders.

So far, so good. We need to carry our share of the load, work wisely and well, and manage our time as good stewards. If we are not careful, however, we will lose something valuable—obeying our good impulses.

Ever had an impulse to phone a friend long distance just to say, "Hi! I'm thinking about you and praying for you!" Did you obey it or let it pass?

Ever had an impulse to compliment some strangers in a restaurant on their well-behaved kids? Or visit a friend in the hospital? Or volunteer to teach a Sunday School class?
A hug for your child?
A compliment with some specifics?
A word of affirmation?
A note in the mail?
The list could go on.

Warmhearted impulses often come from the Holy Spirit. He speaks in a still, small voice or impresses us with a desire to do something good.

I just interrupted this writing to phone a friend in another state who is looking for a job. He wasn't home but I feel better just for obeying the impulse.

Those good impulses may be inner nudgings from the conscience, from a memory about a person's likes or dislikes, from a character quality like kindness or mercy, from the motivation of spiritual gifts or who knows from where else. The important point is that spontaneous urgings for good from within us should be acted on at once. Often they take so little time.

The little points of obedience are just as important as the big ones. Reason: they form our habit patterns.

A few Sundays ago, a friend sitting behind me in worship slipped me a note during the "registration of worshipers." It was kind, encouraging, uplifting and just what I needed at that moment.

After dismissal I thanked him and told him his timing was perfect. Later that same day I was scheduled to deal with a church problem involving a personality conflict. His note gave me the reassurance from the Lord that I needed at that precise moment. He had tears in his eyes as I shared how the Lord used Him.

He obeyed a good impulse, and I was helped. He felt

the joy of obedience and I was more confident that God cared about my need. Whenever I think about this friend, I get a warm feeling on the inside.

Obey your good impulses. Start early in the day. Fit them into the cracks of your tight schedule. The spontaneity will do you good—and your happiness will abound. Who knows how much the Lord will touch others through you?

> Pray for good impulses.
> Work at obeying them.

## Tuesday/Longings

Within each of us are longings—real, vital, God-given. We long for meaning, purpose, love, intimacy, pleasure, enjoyment, satisfaction.

Dr. Larry Crabb in his insightful book, *Inside Out*, divides our longings into three helpful categories.

*Crucial longings* are the desires at the core of our being that only God can satisfy. Eternal salvation, total love, true righteousness, lasting significance and contented security fit well here.

*Critical longings* are the desires that can find fulfillment through human relationships. Human love, acceptance, esteem, influence and all the joys of quality relationships find a place in this category.

*Casual longings* are the desires for physical and material comfort. Pleasant circumstances and passing pleasures fall into this category along with anything that helps us avoid physical discomfort, pain or suffering.

To put it simply,
God meets our crucial longings;
people meet our critical longings;
things meet our casual longings.

I like Dr. Crabb's diagram of three concentric circles that shows how important each of these longings are to us.[1]

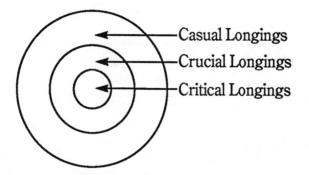

When our casual longings on the surface of our life are not met, we experience manageable discomfort. If the pain level becomes intense (like my bouts with kidney stones), we rush to a hospital for relief. As long as the pain is not life-threatening we recover or adjust and life goes on.

When critical longings are disrupted through severe rejection, divorce, death of a spouse or child, outright rebellion or silent withdrawal, we hurt much more deeply. Initially we may feel lost, immobilized, depressed, rejected, abandoned, betrayed. In time we heal, but often with lasting scars on our personality.

When crucial longings are not met, however, life becomes unspeakably cruel. Without someone who cares fully, something to do that really matters and the reality of eternal salvation, an inner pain cries for satisfaction. Plea-

sures, things, human relationships—even at their best—
will never fully satisfy.

Unmet crucial longings lead to distorted attitudes,
warped behavior and ultimately hell itself. The good news
of the gospel is that Christ meets our crucial longings to a
great extent now and fully in the life to come in heaven.

Some confusion exists about our Lord's role in meeting
critical and casual longings. I have a good friend who has
undergone twenty-five surgeries. She loves the Lord
intensely in the midst of her ongoing suffering. Facing yet
another major surgery, she made an interesting observation.

"Deep inside I have peace," she said. "I know the Lord
is in charge. But in my emotions I am scared to death!"

I asked if "terror" would describe her feelings, and she
agreed. Then we talked about how God always meets our
crucial longings now, but not until eternity does he always
fulfill our other needs.

Disillusionment comes when we expect Christ to work
from the outside in. We want health and wealth first, good
relationships with family and friends next and then a passion for God.

Supernatural energy and genuine maturing in Christ
most often come the opposite way, from the inside out.

A satisfying relationship with God, a passionate love
affair with Christ, comes first. Then His love spills into our
critical connections with family and friends, although most
often with a measure of disappointment.

Pleasant circumstances, good health and material prosperity (casual longings) may or may not come to the committed Christian. Christ meets us in our need, in our suffering, in our cries for help. Sometimes He gives healing,
comfort and prosperity but sometimes in His sovereign
wisdom He does not. We are not in heaven yet!

In the long run, crucial longings that are satisfied by the Holy Spirit will bring us to heaven, and will provide lasting fulfillment of all the others.

Let our hope be confident and sustaining, even when we hurt.

---

Pray for fulfillment of your own crucial longings.
Work at fulfilling other's critical longings.

---

## Wednesday/Energy for the Critical Moment

Stephen emerges out of nowhere. A Greek-speaking Jew who had *not* been with Jesus for three years, he is suddenly named to an important position. (Acts 6:1-6) Quite possibly he was converted on the first Pentecost.

It is clear that Stephen knew the Old Testament Scriptures well before he turned to Christ. His speech in Acts 7 reveals a man familiar with the Word of God.

When he trusted the risen Jesus as his Messiah, his background and childhood training meshed with his new experience of the Holy Spirit to prepare him for the critical moment.

Two phrases in Acts 6 describe this remarkable Christian:

"Full of faith and of the Holy Spirit" (Acts 6:5).
"Full of God's grace and power" (Acts 6:8).

From this fullness came *"great wonders and miraculous signs among the people"* (Acts 6:8) and persuasive preaching and witnessing. In fact his opponents *"could not stand up against his wisdom or the Spirit by whom he spoke"* (Acts 6:10).

The critical moment for Stephen was his witness to the Sanhedrin, the Jewish Council who condemned Jesus. He was energized in such a remarkable way that as he was on trial facing a false charge of heresy, "they saw that his face was like the face of an angel" (Acts 6:15).

After his remarkable defense (Acts 7), Stephen became the first Christian martyr, the first to die for his faith in Jesus. Not only his martyrdom, but also the way he died has inspired Christians through the centuries. While they were stoning him, his last words were "Lord, do not hold this sin against them" (Acts 7:60). Just when he needed it most for God's purpose, the Holy Spirit gave Stephen supernatural energy for the critical moment.

During Paul's first missionary journey, he and Barnabas ran into personal opposition to the gospel (Acts 13:4-12). Bar-Jesus, their critic, also called Elymas, was *"a Jewish sorcerer and false prophet."* He served as an adviser to a prominent Roman official, the proconsul Sergius Paulus. The Roman proconsul was an intelligent man who felt an honest curiosity about the gospel. He sent for the traveling missionaries so that he could personally hear the Word of God.

Sensing the threat to his privileged position, the sorcerer Elymas opposed Paul and Barnabas *"and tried to turn the proconsul from the faith"* (Acts 13:8).

In the critical moment, the Holy Spirit gave Paul supernatural energy for the crisis. *"Then Saul, who was also called Paul, filled with the Holy Spirit, looked straight at Elymas and said, 'You are a child of the devil and an enemy of everything that is right! You are full of all kinds of deceit and trickery. Will you never stop perverting the right ways of the Lord?'"* (Acts 13:9-10).

With prophetic authority Paul pronounced temporary blindness upon the man. *"Immediately mist and darkness came over him, and he groped about, seeking someone to lead him by the hand"* (Acts 13:11). Needless to say, Sergius Paulus, the Roman leader, believed, *"for he was amazed at the teaching of the Lord"* (Acts 13:12.) Just when he needed it most for God's purpose, the Holy Spirit gave Paul supernatural energy for the critical moment.

Our sovereign Lord gives supernatural energy to create a powerful witness in word, in act or even in martyrdom. No one can preplan these critical moments. Our task is to live daily a life that is full of Christ, full of the Holy Spirit.

My circumstances or yours will differ from Stephen's or Paul's. Our critical moments of witness may come when we least expect them. What we can count on is the God of joyful surprises.

Our spiritual gifts may vary from Stephen's or Paul's— and certainly our situations differ. One thing we can feel confident about, the Holy Spirit is the same.

Let's ask our Lord to fill us up and keep us full of the Holy Spirit. Let's deal ruthlessly with substitute fillers that take up His space. Whatever it costs us in personal struggle, let's pursue the fullness of Christ which is our birthright (Col. 2:10).

A Christian who is full of faith and the Holy Spirit can count on supernatural energy for the critical moment.

---

> Pray to be full of faith and the Holy Spirit.
> Work at removing substitute fillers.

## Thursday/Spiritual Gifts

Spiritual gifts are energizers.

Every Christian has one or more spiritual gifts, and through each of them God channels His supernatural energy. For biblical lists of spiritual gifts see Rom. 12:6-8; 1 Cor. 12:27-31; Eph. 4:11.

*"As each one has received a special gift, employ it in serving one another, as good stewards of the manifold grace of God"* Peter admonishes us (1 Pet. 4:10 *NASB*). When we serve others with spiritual gifts we are good stewards, managers of God's grace, distributors of His energizing power.

Like seeds or babies, spiritual gifts start small and grow with proper care. Constant usage, coupled with love and dependence on the Holy Spirit, gradually develop them into effective instruments.

In developing spiritual gifts, the servant of God becomes more and more useful. And it feels so right because God's gifts fit the person. They always match perfectly the personality, temperament and background of each of us.

To some extent our spiritual gifts shape our future. Gifts give guidance as to the type of service the Holy Spirit wants us to pursue. What many of us do not think about is that using spiritual gifts spreads God's energy around.

Hang tough for a short Greek lesson.

In discussing the body of Christ in Eph. 4:16, the apostle Paul used the Greek noun *energeia*, "supernatural energy." It is translated "proper working" (*NASB*) or "does its work" (*NIV*).

The meaning is that each spiritual gift has a measure of supernatural energy for the Body of Christ. Every time a spiritual gift is used it energizes the Church. With this meaning in mind, read this verse in a fresh light:

> From whom [Christ, the head] the whole body,
> being fitted and held together by that which every
> joint supplies, according to [the measure of
> supernatural energy] the proper working of each
> individual part, causes the growth of the body for
> the building up of itself in love" (Eph. 4:16, *NASB*).

From *NIV* it says:

> From him [Christ, the head], the whole body, joined
> and held together by every supporting ligament,
> grows and builds itself up in love, as each part
> [energizes the others] does its work.

So much for the Greek lesson. Let's get on to the practical application.

Christ is the head of His Body. He gives life and direction to the whole Church.

The joints or supporting ligaments, I believe, are the apostles, prophets, evangelists, pastors and teachers listed in Eph. 4:11. These leaders in the church are connectors. They hold the Body together, support and coordinate its parts.

When the gifted leaders fulfill their ministry with excellence, and when most of the people are using their spiritual gifts, the Church is energized. God also causes that Church to grow (Eph. 4:16, Col. 2:19).

Many Christians know from experience that using spiritual gifts is exhilarating. We seldom feel tired while we are using them and, afterward, when the normal human letdown comes, we feel that it was well worth the time and effort.

Spiritual gifts are wonderful presents from God. Unwrap yours, put them to use and watch the release of God's energy.

Three practice steps may help you get started.

Devote your energy.

Develop your ministry.

Discover your gifts.

---

Pray for understanding of spiritual gifts.
Work at using your gifts, strengths and abilities.

---

## Friday/ **Discover Your Gifts**

You can discover your spiritual gifts—with time, patience and a heart to serve God. Four guidelines may help:

*Begin with natural talents, but do not stop there.* Natural talents and spiritual gifts, while not necessarily the same, are vitally connected. The logical starting point of discovering spiritual gifts begins in using natural abilities in the Church. The test of a spiritual gift is whether something supernatural happens as a result of exercising natural talent.

People—at least a few of them—will be attracted to Jesus Christ or built up in their faith when a spiritual gift is at work. Such edification does not occur apart from the Holy Spirit. It is quite possible, however, to possess natural talent without any related spiritual gift.

*Listen to feedback from other Christians.* Other people see us from a fresh slant. Their perspective differs from our self-image. If we rely only upon personal judgment, blind spots in our outlook may cause us to misjudge. Find a few friends who will share constructively in discovering gifts.

The fellowship of God's people also helps in another way. Fellow members of the church ask us to accept responsibilities or perform tasks that they believe fit us. Holding an office or serving in a certain way does not in itself provide a spiritual gift. It simply gives a recognized opportunity for exercising one.

If no gift is discovered in a given assignment, a Christian should find a different task when the term expires. A word of caution; it often takes time and multiplied failures to develop a spiritual gift, but it is more important to have a God-given ministry than a man-made title.

*Learn by success and failure.* Observe the reflection of your gift in the lives of those you live and work with. Notice how they respond. If God repeatedly uses the same ability to help others in a failing situation, you may suspect a spiritual gift.

A young pastor failed miserably in counseling with parishioners, but a few counseling sessions, in apparent defiance of the pattern, proved most successful. Taking a careful look, he found that in each instance those sessions involved teaching. The pastor began to realize that his gift was teaching rather than counseling.

*Feel out your gifts by sensing satisfaction.* Never limit spiritual gifts to the church building. Explore all your God-given interests for possible clues to spiritual gifts.

Using spiritual gifts brings happiness and satisfaction. Exceptions can be cited. The person who grieves the Holy Spirit by sin or self-reliance may experience little joy. A genuine gift may be abused or misused to bring honor to its user instead of Christ. But when the relationship to the Head of the Body is normal, the members enjoy their gifts.

Unless spiritual gifts are used in love they are actually useless (1 Cor. 13). Love makes up for lacks, misunderstandings and failures. Love forgives and counsels and corrects. Love makes the gifts of the Spirit effective rather than offensive.

*"Each one should use whatever gift he has received to serve others, faithfully administering God's grace in its various forms"* (1 Pet. 4:10).

In "administering God's grace" you are giving away supernatural energy. What a joy!

> Pray for insight into your spiritual gifts.
> Work at serving others with them.

## Saturday/**Gifts and Character**

The apostle Paul's stated goal for his ministry was to "present everyone perfect in Christ" (Col. 1:28).

What a goal! What a gift to present to our Lord! People who are complete, mature, perfect "in Christ."

Those last two words are the key to understanding what "perfect" means. Paul is not talking about people with no flaws. He does not mean they lose the all-too-human capacity for mistakes, flubs and sins.

What the great apostle means is that we, in union with Christ, can develop our full potential in gifts and character, and help others do the same. With God-given gifts, strengths, talents and abilities we can grow in ministry skills—sometimes at a steady pace, sometimes in fits and starts.

Gifts grow with time and faithfulness. Gifts produce

spiritual skills and abilities. Gifted people, given the guidance of wise pastors and teachers, develop effective ministries and helpful service to others.

Gifts alone are not enough. Even more important is character—becoming "perfect in Christ."

Character includes the qualities of a Christlike life—integrity, stability, purity, simplicity. Character means developing the fruit of the Spirit—from love to self-control.

Character produces a life marked by righteousness, holiness and the here-and-now-presence of eternal life. Character results from living in union with Christ, and from good training by parents, pastors, teachers and Christian peers.

Our character development depends, in part, on those who have spiritual authority over us. They admonish and teach us with all wisdom. We who submit to their authority and live by their teachings have the opportunity to learn, apply, develop, mature. Always, always, always this progress is "in Christ."

Nourished by the living and written Word of God, guided by the Holy Spirit and discipled by a fellowship of maturing Christians, the inevitable happens. Our gifts and character move toward becoming perfect in Christ.

So many things can retard or destroy the growth—spiritual disease, disunity, distraction, denial and much, much more. Yet the good remains—and it requires supernatural energy that only Christ can give.

> We proclaim him, admonishing and teaching
> everyone with all wisdom, so that we may present
> everyone perfect in Christ. To this end I labor,
> struggling with all his energy, which so powerfully
> works in me" (Col. 1:28-29).

This goal is worthy of our best, and God's power. Let nothing turn us away from it.

> Pray to present others "perfect in Christ."
> Work at developing gifts and character.

## Sunday/Discussion Questions

1. Think of your last week. What good impulses did you have? Did you obey them?
2. Can you identify *your* deepest longings that only Christ can fill? Total love? Eternal salvation? Real significance? Deep meaning? Absolute security? What God-given longings do you feel?
3. Name someone you know who, in your view, is full of faith, the Holy Spirit, God's grace and power? Have you seen supernatural energy at work in a critical moment?
4. From your own experience, give some examples of receiving supernatural energy through other people's spiritual gifts.
5. How did you discover your spiritual gifts? What suggestions do you have for others in their search?
6. What keeps us from using our spiritual gifts more often? How do we learn to use them with greater effectiveness?
7. How can we help others become "perfect in Christ?" What difference do our gifts and character make to other people?

## TEN
# DYNAMIC CHARACTER

God's energy is uplifting, upbuilding, upward moving.

It's healthy, wholesome and dynamic.

It transforms a person where it counts most—character.

Character reflects the way a person is—how he habitually acts and reacts. Character shows what is going on deep inside where only God can see, a person's inner qualities and moral strength.

Godly character is the crown jewel of the Christian life.

## Monday/**Character**

Many people possess knowledge, skills and discipline. Only a few have character.

By character I do not mean merely an interesting personality: "He's quite a character!" Rather, I mean qualities that people most deeply admire: love, compassion, forgiveness, patience, joy, humility and kindness.

Knowledge, skills and hard work bring a qualified kind of admiration, sometimes with a twinge of guilt or jealousy that tags along:

"She is so smart. I wish I had her brains."

"He jogs every morning, works long hours and then keeps his yard looking perfect. How does he do it? It makes me tired just to watch him!"

The inner feeling is, "I *should* do better."

Character, however, brings a deep admiration with joyous feelings of appreciation or love:

"I respect the way he always . . . . "

"She is like that. It's wonderful."

"I remember one time when . . . . "

The inner feeling is, "I *want* to become like that, too."

When people talk about others' knowledge, skill or hard work, they often shake their head. When they speak of uplifting character they almost always smile.

Character, especially Christlike character, makes us want to do better and *be* better. It lifts us. Indeed it's not too much to say that it energizes us.

One of the marks of ability and achievement is that their owners are well aware of the accomplishments. They long to be appreciated, recognized, respected, used by God. When the attitude is right, these longings are normal and healthy.

One of the marks of true character is that people who display it are often unaware of their influence. They simply enjoy loving, serving, giving and seem to think more about Christ and others than about themselves. A remark, an act, a response may impact someone else for good for years to come—and the one who made it never even remembers.

As a pastor I have conducted many funerals. I find that

relatives and close friends talk only a little about professional achievements, financial success and most of the things people work so hard to attain. What they talk most about is the kind of person who was close to them. They tell about incidents that show the best of character.

C.W. Perry, pastor of my home church, often says, "God ministers through our spirit more than through our words." He's right. The spirit of the person makesthe lasting mark. The attitude, motivation, love, self-giving closeness to God—these influence others for a lifetime.

Character grows primarily through a constant connection with God.

> Be imitators of God, therefore, as dearly loved
> children and live a life of love, just as Christ loved
> us and gave himself up for us as a fragrant offering
> and sacrifice to God (Eph. 5:1).

> Therefore, as God's chosen people, holy and dearly
> loved, clothe yourselves with compassion,
> kindness, humility, gentleness and patience (Col.
> 3:12).

> But the fruit of the Spirit is love, joy, peace,
> patience, kindness, goodness, faithfulness,
> gentleness and self-control (Gal. 5:22-23).

Character-building makes all of life richer and better, for you and for everyone around you.

---

Pray for Christlike character.
Work at self-sacrificing love.

### Tuesday/Compassion and Power

What are the crying needs among Christ's people today?

Compassion and power. Not one without the other, but both together.

People who care about people—and who do something about it. That's compassion.

People who love Jesus Christ with all their heart, who communicate His message and who minister with His love so that it transforms other people—that's compassionate power.

Yes, the crying need today is for powerful compassion and compassionate power.

Jess Moody asks some probing questions about our compassion.

*"Did you ever take a real trip down inside the broken heart of a friend? To feel the sob of his soul—the raw, red crucible of emotional agony? To have this become almost as much yours as that of your soul-crushed neighbor? Then, to sit down with him—and silently weep? This is the beginning of compassion."*[1]

Everyone agrees that compassion is a good thing, but power is a little more touchy. Sherri McAdam wrote, *"The only cure for the love of power is the power of love."*[2]

Worldly power tends to corrupt those who wield it. Not so with spiritual power. When genuine, it comes with that strange combination of humility and authority.

Jesus is the best model of compassionate power and powerful compassion—and He wants to build these same qualities into your life.

The Bible speaks of being *"clothed with power"* (Luke 24:49) and says *"clothe yourselves with compassion"* (Col. 3:12).

Compassion and power—the best look for a well-dressed Christian!

---

Pray for compassion and power.
Work at clothing yourself with Christ.

---

## Wednesday/As Jesus Forgave Me

Be kind and compassionate to one another, forgiving each other, just as in Christ God forgave you (Eph. 4:32).

I cannot play the martyr role when I forgive—
    because Jesus did not forgive me that way.
I cannot settle the score first before I forgive—
    because Jesus did not forgive me that way.
I cannot keep a running tally of grievances—
    because Jesus did not forgive me that way.
I cannot forgive with my lips and then bring it up again when I need the advantage of some clout—
    because Jesus did not forgive me that way.
I cannot "forgive" and then tell all the right people about it—
    because Jesus did not forgive me that way.
I cannot go through all the motions of forgiveness and then harbor resentment for weeks, months, years—
    because Jesus did not forgive me that way.
I cannot say, "I forgive, but I can't forget"—
    because Jesus did not forgive me that way.

I can forget the score and erase the tally of rights
and wrongs
      —because Jesus forgave me that way.
I can keep loving and respecting the one who hurt
me
      —because Jesus forgave me that way.
I can look for signs of genuine repentance
      —because Jesus forgave me that way.
I can take the first step to bring about reconciliation
      —because Jesus forgave me that way.
I can forgive and never bring it up again
      —because Jesus forgave me that way.
I can release all the resentment that clings to the
past
      —because Jesus forgave me that way.
I can thaw out the frozen bitterness deep inside and
begin to relieve the other's pain
      —because Jesus forgave me that way.
I can be kind and compassionate, forgiving another
just as in Christ God forgave me (Eph. 4:31-32).

---

Pray for a profound awareness
of God's forgiveness in Christ.
Work at forgiving others
the way that Jesus forgave you.

## Thursday/ The Power of Patience

Have you ever said, "I need more patience" or "Patience is not one of my virtues"? Has anyone ever said to you, "Be patient!" or "You're so impatient!"?

Patience means I can be uncomfortable for a long time—without hating it.

Patience means I can put up with irritable or aggravating people—without chafing.

Patience means I can keep on bearing up in a bad marriage—without divorcing.

Strange as it may sound patience thrives in the crucible of pain and trouble. Just as gold cannot be refined without fire, so patience cannot be learned without the heat of irritation, aggravation and frustration.

*Irritation* . . . is when a man calls you on the telephone about 1:00 A.M. and says, "I want to speak to Joe."

"He doesn't live here," you tell him sleepily.

*Aggravation* . . . is when the same voice calls back at 2:00 a.m. and says, "Are you sure Joe doesn't live there?"

*Frustration* . . . is when a voice calls at 3:00 a.m. and says, "I'm Joe. Do I have any calls?"[3]

God's pleasant surprise is that one of the finest character qualities of the Christian life takes place when you are forced to wait against your choice, when you are uncomfortable and the problem does not go away, when you are under stress and the pressures persist, when you are thrown together with an irregular person and there is no right way to escape.

Patience is not the same as passivity, nor is it weak-willed tolerance. Patience helps you make better decisions. It listens to the people who give sound counsel. It gives sensitivity to the right timing for action instead of moving too soon or too late.

Patience makes you more insightful. It causes you to catch the essential, nonverbal signals that others give.

Patience makes you more trustworthy by avoiding knee-jerking reactions. It includes an alertness to the inner voice of the Holy Spirit instead of to the impulsive outbursts of the flesh.

Patience makes you a better friend, more reliable and less demanding. It opens your eyes to the real potential buried under the person with an exterior of rough edges.

Patience makes you more usable by God. It gives an inner calm to pace your life for maximum usefulness to the Master.

Do you struggle with impatience? The secret of living with a painful person or persevering in a tough situation is to live close to God.

The best way to cope with impatience is to get honest with the Lord Jesus about it when you pray. Give Him control of your inner self, including your impatient feelings.

Be still before Him—for a long time. Wait silently, and never give up.

Patience is a fruit of the Spirit, and fruit does not grow to maturity overnight.

---

Pray for patience.
Work at longsuffering.

---

### Friday/Acceptance

Christ's love, acceptance and forgiveness give a fresh start to each of us when we struggle.

Love and forgiveness, from Christ and from His people, we understand quite well. But acceptance means something different for the Christian than for those in the world system.

In the world system acceptance means I will be tolerant of you no matter what. It often leads to putting a stamp of approval on a harmful or sinful life-style.

Acceptance for the Christian means I will care for you as a person with wonderful potential. I will help you find solutions and point you to the Savior.

The rub comes when the person, often a family member, has hurt me over and over again. This one may be an alcoholic, a drug abuser, someone who runs up my bills and refuses to pay or a spouse who is having an affair.

How does the Christian love, accept and forgive the perennial offender, especially the one who is close to him?

Why not think in terms of being responsible or irresponsible?

I will let you be responsible. And I will not knowingly contribute to your being irresponsible.

I will not try to force you to be responsible by nagging, condemning, scolding, moralizing.

I will not knowingly let you be irresponsible by removing the consequences when you do what is wrong.

I will stand by you, care for you, cry with you; but I will not bail you out time after time after time.

I will not personally judge you, pretending I am your judge instead of God. But neither will I personally provide a shelter for your sin, pretending I am your Savior instead of Christ.

I will love you, accept you, forgive you and give you a fresh start whenever you ask for it.

It's refreshing to share in a fellowship of Christians who love, accept and forgive in the Spirit of Christ!

---

Pray for Christian acceptance.
Work at resisting irresponsibility.

---

## Saturday/ Humility—The Key to Wealth, Honor and Wisdom

Humility is a life empty enough of self that it has plenty of room for God.

Humility seeks the true source of spiritual power. It delights in Christ's presence and gratefully receives supernatural energy for service.

Humility receives remarkable grace from the Lord. It opens the channel for the power flow of the Holy Spirit. When the gifts of God begin their beneficial work, it quietly acknowledges the Giver.

"Clothe yourselves with humility" exhort such strong personalities as the apostle Peter (1 Pet. 5:5) and the apostle Paul (Col. 3:12). Jesus even said that the one who humbles himself like a child is the greatest in the kingdom of heaven (Matt. 18:2-4).

Humble people live free from self-blinding pride. They see themselves for what they are, good and bad. They avoid the hypocrisy in S. Lee Luchansky's definition when he joked that "humility is the ability to act ashamed when you tell people how wonderful you are."[4]

Humility is not putting yourself down
nor clinging to a poor self-image
nor acting like a dog slinking on the ground
when bullied, picked on or in trouble.
Humility is an honest picture of your full stature
when you stand as straight and tall as you can—
next to Jesus Christ.

Humility takes an accurate reading on limitations. It soundly estimates strengths and weaknesses, but flaunts neither one. It can receive a compliment as a gift with a simple "thank you." It will silently praise God for the person who cared enough to express appreciation.

Humility produces a grateful spirit, thanking the Lord for His goodness and greatness, His gifts and blessings.

Humility gladly submits to God and voluntarily yields its rights to those in authority. It sees human authority as the Lord's hand of direction. It remains nondefensive about confrontation and correction.

My friend Bart Mumma once described humility as "the same place our mind was at when we came to Christ." Were we proud when we first knelt at the foot of Christ's cross? No! Words like grateful, broken, overwhelmed, might better fit. Were we not humble and low in the sense of feeling, or even thinking, "I'm not better or greater than anyone else. I'm simply grateful that God so loved me that He touched me with His Son, our Lord Jesus Christ."

Humility never depreciates the value of another person. Quite the opposite, it allows their worth to appreciate. It cherishes the authentic quality of each personality, each talent, each gift, each ability.

Humility rejoices in the success of competitors, even when losing. It gives warm congratulations to the other person who won out for a position, a promotion, a solo or an honor. Humility thanks the Lord for using someone else to fulfill one's own cherished dream.

The Bible makes incredible promises to the humble.

1. Wealth, Deut. 8:10-18; Prov. 22:4; 1 Tim.6:17-19, 1 Kings 3:6-14
2. Deliverance in time of trouble, 2 Sam. 22:28; 2 Chron. 7:13-14; Ps. 147:3,6; Zeph. 2:1-3
3. Salvation, Ps. 149:4-5; Luke 18:9-14
4. Guidance, Ps. 25:8-9
5. Grace, Prov. 3:34; Jas 4:6; 1 Pet. 5:5-6
6. Esteem in God's eyes, Isa. 66:2
7. Christlikeness, Matt. 11:29
8. Wisdom, Prov. 11:2
9. Honor, Prov. 15:33; 18:12; 29:23; Luke 14:7-11
10. Greatness, Matt. 18:2-4

Pursue humility. If you are genuinely humble, people will love you and God will empower you. That's His promise.

---

Pray for humility.
Work on gratitude.

---

## Sunday/ Discussion Questions

1. Think of two or three Christians whom you most admire. What character qualities do you see in their lives? Why is Christlike character so attractive?

2. Do you agree or disagree that compassion and power are crying needs among Christ's people today. Why or why not?

3. How can we increase our appreciation of Christ's forgiving us? How can we remove the barriers to forgive others fully.

4. Review some of the benefits of patience. Which ones do you most desire? What steps can we take to increase patience?

5. How do we accept the person and reject the sin—both at the same time? How does this show up in our actions, attitudes and words?

6. Look up some of the incredible promises God makes to the humble. Why is this character quality so richly rewarded?

7. Share some examples of strong people with a genuine humbleness. How do strength and humility fit together in the life of Jesus?

ELEVEN
# INNER PUSH

How can we become energizers? Like springs of living water, supernatural energy bubbles up from within. How can we pass it on to others?

Too often we meet with stubborn resistance from within ourselves. We have such dull ears, so many bad habits and those ever-present weaknesses.

The good news is that the worst blockades to becoming an energizer can be removed, overcome or dropped. Pushing away inner barriers is sometimes painful but the rewards are great.

One of the finest benefits is that we become the kind of people who give meaning and build high morale in others while enjoying more energy in the process.

## Monday/ Learning to Listen

Listening energizes other people. Something about intense listening brings healing, gives encouragement, offers acceptance, shows love.

Almost everyone agrees. Many people also struggle to listen well. Most would like to listen better.

If the subject turns to one of our favorite topics— sports, work, people news—we catch every word. If the talk turns to something we could care less about, our mind begins to wander.

Sometimes it can get embarrassing. Suddenly the other person says something or asks a question, and we find ourselves stumbling and fumbling for an acceptable response. We hate to admit our mind was somewhere else while they were talking.

Trying harder to listen better never seems quite enough. I tried for years to improve—and failed—until I discovered a simple insight. Somehow I was led into the practice of silently praying for the person who is talking to me. Far from interrupting my listening, I found that I tuned in with new power.

Since we think faster than we listen, silent prayer does not interfere with hearing. Quite the opposite, prayer opens new dimensions in our mind and spirit.

> We listen with love.
> We listen with genuine interest.
> We listen with our spirit.
> We listen with the Holy Spirit's help.
> We listen with caring in our eyes.

Suddenly we hear with sensitive ears. We hear with warm hearts.

The surprise is how people respond.

> "Thank you for listening to me."
> "You're such a good listener."

Another tip or two.
Ask some objective questions.

> "When did that happen?"
> "Who else was involved?"
> "Which came first?"

Search for feelings.

> "Why is it so important to you?"
> "How did that make you feel?"
> "What else are you feeling?"

Watch for problems and think of solutions.

> "From what you're saying, it sounds to me like the real problem is . . . What do you think?"
> "A couple of possible solutions that come to my mind are . . . What other ones do you think of?"

Pray quietly for the one who is talking.
Listen with fresh love.
Ask, search, watch, think.
Then stand in amazement as the Holy Spirit opens your spiritual ears.

---

Pray for spiritual ears.
Work at praying for the one who is speaking.

---

## Tuesday/Good Habits

Few things lead to more energy, productivity and personal growth than good habits.

Few things lead to more lethargy, decline and decay than bad habits.

All of life tends to fall into habit patterns—ways of thinking, feeling and doing. Good habits lead to incredible power to influence others. Bad habits lead to devastating loss.

Building good habits is never easy. My wife, Nancy, once made a tongue-in-cheek observation on the subject. *"Half the time they're more trouble than they're worth. They're too much work. It's easier to have bad ones. Good habits take discipline!"*

Why is it that bad habits come so easy and good habits come so hard? Why is it so easy to slide out of a good habit and slip into a bad one? I have heard of backsliding all my life, but I have never heard of "front-slipping" or "forward sliding."

Have you ever questioned the basic sinfulness of human nature? A sure sign of depravity is that good habits take training and bad habits need only neglect.

So why bother? Why put out the effort to build good habits and break bad ones?

- Because habits make a person likeable or disgusting.
- Because habits shape life-styles for better or for worse.
- Because habits bring success or failure.
- Because habits make our work useful or useless.
- Because habits lead us closer to Christ or drive us further away.

Okay, okay, so much for the sermon. We all agree that good habits are a necessary nuisance—especially in other people. It was Mark Twain who quipped, "Nothing so needs reforming as other people's habits."[1]

Two words of caution. First, any habit, no matter how good, must submit to Christ. Pursuing a self-righteous habit that replaces an intimate relationship with our Lord Jesus leads to legalism and a judgmental attitude.

Second, habits must never squelch warm impulses, good urges or Spirit-directed intuition. Being spontaneous in the Lord has its benefits, too.

Habits grow from character. A person whose character is marked by love, integrity, honesty and perseverance *will* have good habits.

It's also a two-way street. While character qualities such as the fruit of the Spirit (Gal. 5:22-23) produce good habits, it is likewise true that good habits build character.

"Sow an act and you reap a habit. Sow a habit and you reap a character. Sow a character and you reap a destiny."[2]

Most of the commands in Scripture, when obeyed regularly, lead to good habits.

I once read in the newspaper that it takes about three weeks to form a new habit. Practice it daily for twenty-one days, then repeat it as often as needed to reinforce it. (Just a tip).

When centered in our Lord Jesus Christ, good habit patterns lead us to a life that pleases God.

---

Pray for Spirit-formed character.
Work at building good habits.

## Wednesday/ **Weaknesses**

Everyone has strengths and weaknesses. Everyone.

The only person who ever lived without any personality or spiritual weaknesses was our Lord Jesus. The Bible explicitly states that He had physical weaknesses and was tempted in every way, just as we are (Heb. 4:14-16).

Our weaknesses are limitations, and overcoming limitations is the primary task in achieving excellence and becoming energizers.

- Physical weaknesses
- Emotional weaknesses
- Intellectual weaknesses
- Ability weaknesses
- Personality weaknesses

One person is prone to sickness. Another lives with damaged emotions from childhood abuse. Another has learning handicaps. Yet another lacks talent or a winning personality. We all have weaknesses.

Just after exulting that God *"made his light shine in our hearts to give us the light of the knowledge of the glory of God in the face of Christ,"* the Bible quickly adds, *"But we have this treasure in jars of clay"* (2 Cor. 4:6-7).

Clay pots. Clay jars. Clay pitchers. Clay earthenware. We come in all kinds of shapes, sizes and capacities but we are all clay.

Breakable.

Cracked.

Worn.

Chipped.

Weak.

So what are we to do? Consider a few suggestions.

### 1. Face up to our weaknesses.

Admit them. Accept them. Laugh at them. Tolerate them. Put up with them. Work around them. But never, never expect perfection in ourselves or in others. We are mortals, not gods.

### 2. Work on improving them.

Many weaknesses can be improved upon, if not overcome entirely.

Orthodontists can straighten crooked teeth.

Competent counselors can relieve emotional pain.

Good teachers can improve academic skills in slow learners.

Caring managers can teach new job skills.

Loving friends can bring out the best in any personality.

One of our major tasks is to expose our weaknesses to those who can help us improve.

### 3. Find people whose strengths compensate for our weaknesses.

Every church, every organization, every human association needs people working in their areas of strength. A major key to an energized church or company is to let workers do what they do best.

On a personal level, each of us needs to serve where we do best and look for others to serve where we are weak. Teamwork is essential for progress. Working together we maximize our strengths and minimize our weaknesses.

### 4. Ask Christ to use our weaknesses for His glory.

This final suggestion is so humbling—even humiliating—that we feel reluctant to pursue it. Our pride drives us to hide our weaknesses, cover them, even lie about them. The last thing we want to do is expose them.

Wait a minute. *"We have this treasure in jars of clay to show that this all-surpassing power is from God not from us"* (2 Cor. 4:7).

Simply ask the Lord to let the glistening of the treasure shine through the cracks in the clay pot. Ask that these imperfect vessels of ours spill out the riches of God's all-surpassing power.

*"God chose the weak things of the world to shame the strong. He chose the lowly things of this world and the despised things—and the things that are not—to nullify the things that are, so that no one may boast before him"* (1 Cor. 1:27-29).

Do you feel weak, limited, even incompetent? Listen to the Lord's voice. *"My grace is sufficient for you, for my power is made perfect in weakness"* (2 Cor. 12:9).

Then respond in humbleness—even if it is embarrassing, *"Therefore I will boast all the more gladly about my weaknesses, so that Christ's power may rest on me. That is why, for Christ's sake, I delight in weaknesses, in insults, in hardships, in persecutions, in difficulties. For when I am weak, then I am strong"* (2 Cor. 12:9-10).

When we always look for the treasure in the clay pot we will rejoice in our riches and be thankful for *any kind of container* that will hold them.

---

> Pray for awareness of Christ's treasure within.
> Work at overcoming or accepting
> the weaknesses of our clay pots.

### Thursday/ Little Deaths

For twenty centuries—and more often in this one than any other—Christians have given their lives as martyrs for the faith. They are the heroes, the great ones, the members of Christ's hall of fame.

What's overlooked is that some others around them did in fact "shrink from death."

A few, under pressure, denied Christ.

More, thinking they were smart, stopped Christian activities "temporarily" until the heat was off.

Many, half-hearted and self-serving, conformed to the current persecuting culture. They succeeded so well that there was insufficient evidence to convict them.

All of these loved their lives too much.

In a chapter of the Bible on spiritual warfare (Rev. 12) stands a startling statement. *"They did not love their lives so much as to shrink from death"* (Rev. 12:11). What does it take for Christians not to "love their lives so much" that they deny Christ in word or action when the power to conform to this world is at its highest?

My guess is that it takes not shrinking from little deaths day by day.

It takes a little death—dying to self and to sin—to overcome Satan anytime.

It takes a little death—dying to comfort and social conformity—to speak a word of testimony for Christ to nonbelievers.

It takes a little death—simply not to love our lives so much.

What are the advantages of not shrinking from death—even little deaths?

- We overcome the adversary, *"that ancient serpent called the devil or Satan, who leads the whole world astray"* (Rev. 12:9).
- We share the sufferings of our Lord Jesus Christ. *"I want to know Christ and the power of his resurrection and the fellowship of sharing in his sufferings, becoming like him in his death"* (Phil. 3:10).
- We prepare ourselves for the resurrection from the dead. Paul follows the verse above with his big goal: *"and so, somehow, to attain to the resurrection from the dead"* (Phil. 3:11).
- We cause heaven to rejoice. Note the next verse in Revelation: *"Therefore rejoice, you heavens and you who dwell in them!"* (Rev. 12:12).

Little deaths! *"I die every day—I mean that,"* wrote Paul (1 Cor. 15:31).

Little deaths—to sin, to self-protection, to self-indulgence, to personal comfort—prepare the way to pass the big test when it comes: And these same little deaths qualify us for the supernatural energy that wins in spiritual warfare against the adversary.

Do you want to be an overcomer? Do you want to win over the evil one? Do not love your life so much as to shrink from death.

Jesus said it best. *"For whoever wants to save his life will lose it, but whoever loses his life for me will find it"* (Matt. 16:25).

---

Pray for courage.
Work at *not* loving your life so much.

---

## Friday/ The Hidden Demand

Every one of us has legitimate inner longings—desires for love, meaning, significance, security, intimacy, relationship, pleasure.[3] What's illegitimate is that we build selfish self-protective behaviors around *unmet* longings to protect us from pain.

We respond with anger, resentment, bitterness and rage. Or we go the route of rigid self-discipline, careful rule-keeping, legalistic righteousness while holding others at arm's length and violating the command to love. Or we indulge in blame-shifting, rationalizing, self-justifying, excuse-making. Each of these patterns hinder us from becoming energizers.

Behind the inner pain is a demand, often a hidden demand. We demand not to hurt any more. We demand that our desires be satisfied, our longings fulfilled, our pain soothed.

We demand it of God, of others, of ourselves—as soon as possible or at least within a reasonable period of time. Certainly it must come before heaven—no matter what it takes or who gets hurt.

The problem with the demand is that
it drains away our energy,
it puts God on our string like a puppet,
it puts our own desires and behaviors before others,
it is incredibly stubborn, self-seeking and self-serving.

The hidden demand masquerades as something healthy—self-esteem, wounded justice, service to God, to name a few. It even makes us feel good—for a little while. In turn, we dismiss it as normal and healthy.

The Bible has other terms for this hidden, inner

demand—pride, the sin nature, the flesh, the body of sin, dead men's bones.

How do we deal with this inner, selfish demand? Here are ten painful, but healing, steps.

1. Face up to the hidden demand within that unmet longings be fulfilled.
2. Go ahead and hurt. Learn to live with the pain of disappointing relationships, personal failure, damaged emotions, old regrets and unfulfilled needs.
3. Acknowledge that God alone has the love, power and grace to meet our deepest longings, and some of His fulfillment and relief—perhaps much of it—is promised for heaven.
4. Repent of selfish self-protective behaviors that violate Christ's command to love. Self-protection always hinders our love of God and others—always.
5. Drop the demand for relief and fulfillment. Give Christ both the pain and the unmet longings. Release self-will, self-seeking, stubborn pride. This calls for a death to the old self.
6. Put trust in Christ alone for the working out of His sovereign will for our lives.
7. Ask the Holy Spirit to fill the void caused when the demand is dropped.
8. Discover self-giving love, a desire to serve, a new measure of grace, inner freedom, fresh energy. The pain is not gone but the energy-draining demand is.
9. Pray that God will make giving up "demandingness" a life-changing event.
10. Work on changing old habit patterns of self-protective behavior. Write out the opposite

of each self-protective behavior in terms of self-giving love. Pray over this list daily.

Guess what happens next? Losing your life, you find it.

---

Pray for insight and conviction
about your own form of hidden demands.
Work on repentance and long-lasting
faith in Christ.

---

## Saturday/Meaning, Morale and Momentum

A deep, motivational, driving force in a person's life is the presence of *meaning*.

It is not enough for us just to exist or even to live comfortably. We long for something significant to do, something worthwhile to achieve, something important to believe in. We thrive on meaning.

Meaning answers the question, Why?

Why do I have value?

Why does life have purpose?

Why does a specific job or task have importance?

People feel more motivated and energized and will work longer and harder when they understand *why* and not just *how*. Meaning gives dignity, worth, value, purpose, direction.

When a group of people such as a church or denomination agree on the meaning of their life together, *morale* begins to build. The more intensely they agree on their purpose, goal or mission, the more excited they become.

High morale thrives on expectancy, warm relationships and God-given achievement. Where morale is high a beautiful spirit of trust, giving and love flows among the people. Tenderness, appreciation and caring can be felt everywhere. Problems and conflicts are worked through with patience and wisdom.

High morale causes people to give their best. When people give their all, the result is excellence. In an upward cycle, the more people see excellence the more they take a holy pride in their church, class or group.

With meaning and morale in place a series of God-given achievements leads to an exhilarating sense of *momentum*. We feel part of a movement. It is moving at an enjoyable pace, and sometimes exciting speed. Momentum energizes everyone.

Think back to the development of a new denomination, perhaps your own.

In the beginning a Holy Spirit-inspired leader gave fresh *meaning* to the gospel, the Scripture or some portion of God's revealed truth. This meaning captured people's lives and they found Christ or discovered His grace in a fresh, energizing way.

Their glorious experiences led to a confident sense of joy, understanding and great value. They simply could not keep it to themselves. The leaders and virtually all of the followers began to share, witness, preach, publish, persuade and plant churches everywhere possible.

As others caught the meaning, the vision of the group crystallized. Expectations rose. They bound themselves together for a great purpose, sparing no energy to reach their common goals.

*Morale* was high, in spite of suffering and setbacks. It seemed that nothing could stop them.

This sense of invincibility under God, this awareness of movement, even rapid movement toward the Lord's goals, created *momentum*. As the momentum kept building a denomination was born, and grew and touched thousands or even millions of lives.

In His sovereign will, God uses some people to show us meaning, others to build our morale and yet others to create momentum. A few gifted leaders—very few—generate all three.

Meaning, morale and momentum—where do you fit?

---

Pray for meaning, morale and momentum.
Work at generating at least one of the three.

---

## Sunday/Discussion Questions

1. Share some tips to becoming a better listener. What is it about some people that make us feel so accepted, comfortable and loved?
2. Why is it that bad habits come so easy and good habits come so hard?
3. How can Christ use our weaknesses for His glory? What is the balance between overcoming weaknesses and delighting in them?
4. Share some examples of "little deaths" for Christ's sake. In an age that stresses self-love, is it possible to love our lives too much?
5. Do you agree or disagree that a hidden demand for satisfaction of our inner longings is sinful? When does God-given desire turn into selfish demand?

6. Have you ever been part of a movement, church or denomination that experienced meaning, morale and momentum? If so, describe it. If not, what can you do to help?

TWELVE

# ETERNAL PULL

Hope is energizing—and the Christian holds the greatest confidence of anyone for the eternal future.

A two-age perspective—now and then—kept in careful balance is a rich asset. We know that this world and this life are not the end.

No matter how bad things may get, we know that one day our reigning King will come to the rescue. Those who are His will rise to reign with Him in resurrected, immortal bodies.

This truth does not mean we ignore the here and now. Quite the opposite. Because we must all face judgment, we live carefully and wisely in this world, making the most of every opportunity.

It's true. There is hell to avoid and heaven to gain. This truth alone makes it worth all the grace we can receive and all the discipline we can muster. A healthy focus on our eternal future lifts our spirits and deepens our determination.

## Monday/Two Age-Perspective

What every Christian needs is a balanced, two age-perspective. We need to see this present age with all of its possibilities and problems in light of the age to come. We need the reality of eternity to inform our thinking and our feelings about today.

The Bible divides all of history into two ages: this present age and the age to come.

Each age is ruled by a separate kingdom—one temporal and one eternal, the kingdom of darkness and the kingdom of light.

This present age is evil, dominated by the world system that leaves out God, the sinful nature with its bent toward sinning and the influence of Satan and his demons. Shorthand expressions for these three deceivers are "the world, the flesh and the devil."

The age to come is ruled by the Lord God Himself. It is a kingdom of light, life and love. Christ reigns here in a kingdom of righteousness, peace and joy in the Holy Spirit. This is the eternal kingdom.

The two kingdoms are in conflict.

The good news is that the age to come has invaded this present evil age. The kingdom of light is penetrating the kingdom of darkness. This invasion began in Old Testament times. God gave His word—promises, warnings and fulfillment. He called out a people for Himself, imperfect as they were.

In spite of setbacks, the invasion progressed onward.

In the coming to earth of our Lord Jesus Christ, the kingdom of light greatly increased. The decisive battle was fought and won in the cross and Resurrection. In one sense the war is won, although many other battles will be fought before it is over.

The future, the age to come, the kingdom of light continues to win its victories in this present evil age dominated by the kingdom of darkness. It is accurate to speak of the presence of the future.[1] What God planned for the coming age has become present now in Christ.

Each age, each kingdom has its own values. Those who live only in this present, evil age share the values of the world system, make provision for the sinful nature and are influenced by the evil one.

We who belong to the age to come must live in a world dominated by this present evil age, but our values and deepest desires are vastly different. We march to a different drumbeat. We love a different King. We yield to a different Spirit. We proclaim a different message. We hold a different hope.

The age to come will reach its consummation when King Jesus returns. The kingdom of darkness will be dispelled, its adherents judged and its values put to an end. The kingdom of light will last forever.

A balanced, two-age perspective means that we see everything with eternity in view. The age to come, the kingdom of light, the King of kings rules our thinking and our feeling.

When we let the age to come rule our lives, our thoughts and our emotions, then we will have supernatural energy. Seeing the reality of the age to come gives hope. And hope always energizes.

Always.

---

Pray for a balanced, two-age perspective.
Work at living now in Christ's kingdom.

## Tuesday/ The King to the Rescue

*Revelation*, the last book of the Bible, pictures the awesome reality of the Antichrist and the Great Tribulation.

The Bible does not fully reveal in advance the precise time of the Great Tribulation nor the exact identity of the Antichrist. However, the Scriptures are unmistakably clear when it comes to identifying our Savior. God leaves us with no questions about the Lord Jesus Christ who has come and will come again.

He pitched His tent among us for thirty-three years, and then was hammered to a cross. He gave His life in sacrifice for our sin and rose again from the dead in order to give you and me eternal life. This same Jesus is clearly revealed as God the Son, the Lord of the universe, the Savior of all who will repent and believe.

He is coming again! The most dramatic picture in the Bible of Christ's return in conquering power is Rev. 19:11-16. Heaven opens. Charging out on a white stallion rides a conquering King. His eyes blaze with fury at the injustice done to His people. His bejeweled crowns signal the authority and kingdoms which rightfully belong to Him.

Take a second look! This is no parade. What you see is the Winning Warrior. His blood-spattered robe ripples in the wind of His charging steed. His sword strikes the mortal blow to His enemies.

Armies of angels and saints—riding behind Him on their white horses—carry no weapons. They are following in a gigantic victory celebration!

In one fell swoop He takes command of the conquered forces gathered against Him on earth, smashing their injustice and coming to the rescue of His faithful saints. With full force He treads the winepress of the wrath of God Almighty.

The hymn writer puts it in words we sing, but seldom understand.

> "Mine eyes have seen the glory of the coming of
> the Lord;
> He is trampling out the vintage where the grapes of
> wrath are stored;
> He hath loosed the fateful lightning of His terrible
> swift sword;
> His truth is marching on."[2]

Do you see who He is? Four names reveal the true nature of the rider on the white horse.

*1. He "is called Faithful and True"* (Rev. 19:11).
Only one man fits that description in perfection. We crucified Him.

*2. "He has a name written on him that no one knows but he himself"* (Rev. 19:12).
Only He knows the wonderful and awesome realities of His full person and work. He understands far more than has been revealed to us. Someday, after the Final Victory, He will share even more of Himself with us.

*3. "His name is the Word of God."* (Rev. 19:13).
Only He is the living, energizing, creating, revealing, redeeming, threatening, judging one—all embodied in the holy rider on the white stallion.

*4. "On his robe and on his thigh he has this name written: KING OF KINGS AND LORD OF LORDS"* (Rev. 19:16).
Only one name can his enemies see—and it speaks of awesome power, supreme authority, striking force.

He conquers—for a purpose: *"that at the name of Jesus every knee should bow, in heaven and on earth and under the earth, and every tongue confess that Jesus Christ is Lord, to the glory of God the Father"* (Phil. 2:10-11).

The German theologian and preacher, Helmet Thielicke sums it up.

> One day the eyes which were wild with hatred will have to see Him as He is.
> One day the fists which clenched against Him will open in a gesture of worship.
> One day the knees which were stiff and independent will bow before Him.
> This will be the second Easter of His coming again.
> This will be the moment when faith may see what it has believed and unbelief will have to see what it has not."[3]

The King is coming to the rescue! Whose side are you on?

---

> Pray for Christ's return.
> Work to be prepared.

---

## Wednesday/A Resurrected Body

Christians live with an eternal pull toward the life to come. God has put eternity in their hearts.

The apostle Paul felt this creative tension when he wrote from prison: *"I am torn between the two: I desire to depart and be with Christ, which is better by far; but it is more necessary for you that I remain in the body"* (Phil. 1:23-24).

An inexpressible joy and quiet confidence permeates the funeral of every committed Christian. When these physical bodies enter the sleep of death, our eternal souls are immediately with the Lord Jesus. "To be absent from the body [is] to be present with the Lord" (2 Cor. 5:8, *KJV*).

Theologians call this "the intermediate state." What a boring term. Jesus called it "paradise" (Luke 23:43). Much better.

Some Christians do not grasp the power and wonder of their final state—a resurrected *body*. Their thinking is stuck at the intermediate—a disembodied soul floating around in clouds strumming a harp.

Who wants it? Who wants to live for all eternity with consciousness but no body in which to express it? Who wants to float in eternal bliss with nothing to do but sit around heaven all day? If that kind of existence is so great how come everyone works so hard to stay in this frail body? Why do we pay doctors and hospitals such handsome fees to keep body and soul together? Frankly, I'm not interested in spending eternity without a resurrected body.

Okay, I can put up with it for a little while. I know what the Word of God says. Let me repeat it again *"To be absent from the body [is] to be present with the Lord"* (2 Cor. 5:8 *KJV*). The good part of this verse is being present with the Lord. Being with Jesus I will like. But absent from the body? That's just a temporary state of affairs until that "Great Gettin' Up Mornin'" when all of God's people will rise from the dead in resurrected bodies.

What will our resurrected bodies be like? The strongest teaching of Scripture is that they will be like the resurrected body of our risen Lord Jesus (Phil. 3:20-21; 1 John 3:2). Think about Jesus' body and actions after the first glorious Easter, and what this may mean for us.

- Suited to the environment of the new heavens and new earth (1 Cor. 15:42-44; 1 Thess. 4:13-18).
- Perfected in personality—you will receive a new name, symbolizing that the "real you" God intended will come through (Rev. 3:17).
- Freed from the limitations of this physical body (Phil. 3:20-21; 1 John 3:2).
- Able to appear or disappear, even behind locked doors (Luke 24:36-40; John 20:19-20)
- Able to disguise appearance, voice, mannerisms (Luke 24:13-35).
- Able to eat—my guess is *without* getting fat— (Luke 24:40-42).
- Able to teach, share, enjoy personal relationships (Luke 24:44-49; John 20:21-30).
- Able to communicate fully with Christ and His angels (Rev. 3:21; 1 Cor. 6:3).
- Able to see God without distraction or destruction (1 John 3:2).
- Able to worship with full concentration and involvement (Rev. 5:13).
- Able to reflect and radiate God's glory (Col. 3:4; Matt. 13:43).
- Never get sick (Rev. 21:4).
- Never get tired or sleepy (Rev. 21:22-25).
- Never die; immortal; death-proof (1 Cor. 15:42; Rev. 21:4).

I know one thing. This is too good to miss!

"Everyone who has this hope in him purifies himself, just as he is pure" (1 John 3:3).

Make a purity inspection of your life now. You don't want to be disqualified for a resurrected body then!

> Pray for excitement about the
> resurrected body.
> Work at purifying yourself as
> He is pure.

## Thursday/Books and the Book

Picture in your mind the Great White Throne of the last judgment. Can you see it? It rises into view, white like a glistening pearl with luster and brilliance.

Here comes the Judge, taking His seat on the awesome throne. As He steps closer, gasps are heard.

Nail prints. . .in His hands.

Gaping scars. . .around the holes in His feet.

Open wound. . .from the spear that pierced His side.

The Judge is none other than God the Son, the merciful one who sacrificed Himself on our behalf.

Every person has an inevitable appointment with judgment.

Christians will stand before the judgment seat of Christ (Rom. 14:10; 2 Cor. 5:10).

Others will stand before the Great White Throne (Rev. 20:11-15).

No missing this appointment,
no escape,
no place to hide,
no way out—
everyone will give account to God (Rom.
14:12).

No acquittals are granted on the great Judgment Day.
Acquittals are available—but only in advance. The
Judge and the Savior are one and the same Lord. He is
handing out pardons to all who yield their lives to Him in
genuine repentance and faith—but only now, not then.

The ground is level in only two places—the foot of the
cross and the base of the throne. The "great" of the earth
will be there—presidents; kings and queens; dictators;
famous athletes and entertainers; noted authors and edu-
cators; prominent scientists and researchers; winners of
Nobel peace prizes, honorary doctorates, Oscars, Gram-
mies, Emmys.

The "small" people will also be there—all the people of
the earth whose names will never go down in a history
book or make the newspaper or win any awards. But the
Lord knows every one. Every single person will keep this
appointment with the Judge.

At the command of Judge Jesus, the angels bring out
the book, a careful record of every act and every word.

*Volume I. The book of God's law* (Rev. 2:5-6,12).

With tender grief in His voice, Jesus begins to read. He
looks up and with a tear in His eye, calls you by name. "It
says here that you used my Name as a swear word when
you got mad. Is that true?"

Before you can answer, like a flashback a huge screen
rolls before you and in living color you relive the memories

of all the times you cursed and swore, and never bothered to ask forgiveness and seek cleansing.

The Judge's eyes drop to the page and scan a few lines. "The books say you lied. . .not once but often."

The flashbacks roll again—all the times you lied and deceived people. You stand speechless, without excuse.

*Volume II. The book of conscience* (Rom. 2:14-15).
*Volume III. The book of secrets* (Eccles. 12:14, Rom. 2:16).
*Volume IV. The book of motives* (1 Cor. 4:5).
*Volume V. The book of careless words* (Matt. 12:36-37).
*Volume VI. The book of money* (Luke 16:13-15).
*Volume VII. The book of broken relationships* (Matt. 7:1-2).

One book stands by itself, separate from all the others. Seven times the New Testament refers to it, *The Book of Life* (Phil. 4:3; Rev. 3:5; 13:8; 17:8; 20:12,15; 21:27).

In the Book of Life will be the names of those who have trusted Jesus Christ as Lord and Savior. In the ancient world of Bible times every city and ruler had a book listing all the living citizens. When someone died, his name was removed. In a similar way the names in the Book of Life are the living, active citizens of God's kingdom.[4]

In Christ, you can have confidence in God's love (1 John 4:15-17).

Take a moment to answer three crucial questions.

*1. Is your name in the Book of Life?*
If you are uncertain, acknowledge *"that Jesus is the Son of God"* (1 John 4:15). Do this in the presence of your family, your friends and your church. Ask your pastor for direction.

### 2. Are you sure?

You can know the full assurance of salvation. Read 1 John over and over underlining the words *joy, confidence* and *know*. Ask the Holy Spirit to renew your joy and restore your confidence until you know for sure.

### 3. Is there enough evidence to prove it?

Let Christ work in you until all the volumes of the books of heaven reveal that indeed your name is written in the Lamb's Book of Life.

---

> Pray for your name to be
> written in the Lamb's Book of Life.
> Work for enough evidence to prove it.

---

## Friday /Why Hell?

God does not want anyone to go to hell. *"He is patient with you, not wanting anyone to perish, but everyone to come to repentance"* (2 Pet. 3:9).

So why hell?

As a young pastor I went through a tough time of questioning. *"How can I put together an eternal hell and a loving God?"*

Then I asked myself another question. *"Do I believe what Jesus taught about heaven and hell is true?"*

I read every Bible verse in which Jesus spoke about hell. I was shocked how often He spoke about outer darkness, weeping and gnashing of teeth, eternal fire and everlasting punishment. Even the Sermon on the Mount with its famous ethical teachings contains undeniable references to hell (Matt. 5:29-30). Most of the rest of the Bible said little about it except the last book, *The Revelation of Jesus Christ.*

I knew that I believed what Jesus taught. He was the supreme example of love and the only one who came from the Other Side. He knew, and He cared enough to warn us.

I had other questions. Was Jesus' picture language a symbol? The disturbing answer that came to me was that symbols in the Bible only portray realities that are greater than the symbols. I found no comfort in thinking that hell might be worse than the graphic descriptions of our Lord Jesus.

Was hell temporary? I liked that idea but could find no convincing evidence in the Scriptures.

So why hell?

*Hell honors human choice.* God gives us the dignity of decision, even if we choose to reject Christ. A rebellious arrogance prefers to "do it my way" and go to hell. Christ does not force Himself down anyone's throat—not His free gift of salvation, not eternal life, not even heaven. Billy Graham reminds us that "God takes no delight in people going to hell. He never meant that anyone would ever go to hell. He created hell for the devil and his angels. But if we persist in going the devil's way and obeying the devil instead of God, we are going to end up there."[5]

*Hell confines evil.* Anyone can see that evil is rampant in our world. In the coming age it will be shrunk into one place. Hell will have a total absence of God and of good. Think about it—no goodness at all, ever.

*Hell provides justice.* Most of us can understand why Hitler, Stalin or a deliberate mass murderer would go to hell. What we miss is that, to be just and to fulfill His role as Judge of the universe, God must punish each of us for our sins. Our only escape comes by taking refuge in Christ's death on the cross for us and our sins. *"God made him who had no sin to be sin for us, so that in him we might become the righteousness of God"* (2 Cor. 5:21).

*Hell motivates with a healthy fear.* I was traveling down I-99 Freeway between Sacramento and Fresno on a quiet Sunday morning. Very little traffic was on the road. I glanced in my rear view mirror to see a California Highway Patrol car coming up behind me fast. A quick look at my speedometer showed I was driving too fast. Out loud I said, *"I'm dead."*

Fear, or was it terror, raced through my whole nervous system. I slowed down. The patrol car came up behind me and stayed. I changed lanes to the right with a careful signal. He stayed in my blind spot for what seemed like forever. I kept waiting for the red light or siren. I knew that I was guilty and deserved the punishment that was coming. Then his patrol car inched past me and kept going.

He showed mercy and I was warned. Believe me, I felt fresh motivation to drive slower all the way to Fresno. Healthy fear has its benefits.

Motivation is a powerful form of energy. In all of life, here and hereafter, God promises rewards and punishments as motivators. We ignore them to our own peril.

The question now changes from, *"Why hell?"* to *"Why do we so seldom teach and preach about hell?"* A defective gospel only produces crippled Christians.

---

Pray for a healthy fear of hell.
Work to understand God's justice.

---

## Saturday/**Hooked on Heaven**

Something about anticipating great rewards is energizing.

Olympic athletes reach for hidden reserves of energy in seeking a gold medal. Pro football players show amazing ferocity and skill for a Super Bowl ring. Concert pianists practice hours each day for the applause and acclaim of crowds and critics.

The greatest of all rewards is heaven. The Bible uses an array of tantalizing images to portray the wonders of heaven.

- Heaven is a lovely home (John 14:2).
- Heaven is a better country (Heb. 11:13-16).
- Heaven is a beautiful city (Heb. 11:10,16; Rev. 21:1-2).
- Heaven is a marriage feast (Rev. 19:7-9).
- Heaven is a paradise regained (Rev. 22:1-6.)

What makes heaven so desirable, in part at least, is what will *not* be there (Rev. 21:1-27):

- No death.
  No cemeteries. No funeral homes. No caskets.
- No grief.
  No mourning. No crying. No tears.
- No pain.
  No surgery. No drugs. No hospitals.
- No danger.
  No violence. No war. No criminals.
- No impurity.
  No perversion. No immorality. No filth.

What makes heaven so attractive is what *will* be there:

- We will see God face-to-face there (1 Cor. 13:12; 1 John 3:2; Rev. 22:4).
- We will reign with Him forever and ever there (Rev. 22:5).
- We will worship His majesty there (Rev. 4:1-11; 5:1-14; 6:9-15).
- We will enjoy eternal rewards there (Matt. 25:34; 2 Cor. 5:1- 10; Rev. 20:11-13).
- We will function in a powerful, imperishable, resurrected body there (1 Cor. 15:42-44).
- We will serve God there (Rev. 22:3).

Do you want to be there?
You don't have to be there (Rev. 21:8).
But you can be there!

I am the Alpha and the Omega, the Beginning and the End. To him who is thirsty I will give to drink without cost from the spring of the water of life. He who overcomes will inherit all this, and I will be his God and he will be my son.
—Rev. 21:6-7

Whoever is thirsty, let him come; and whoever wishes, let him take the free gift of the water of life"
—Rev. 22:17.

Are you thirsty? Ask Jesus to satisfy you with living water. The final satisfaction and the finest reward come in heaven.
Be there!

---

Pray to be hooked on heaven.
Work at anticipating your reward.

## Sunday/Discussion Questions

1. Do you believe that most Christians have a balanced, two-age perspective? Why or why not?
2. How can we prepare for Christ's second coming?
3. Do you picture your future in heaven as living in a disembodied soul or in a resurrection body? Which does the Bible teach? How can we purify ourselves?
4. Do you agree or disagree that the Christian will face judgment? How do you reconcile Jesus' promise that the Christian "*does not come into judgment*" (John 5:24, *NASB*) with the fact that Christians "*must all appear before the judgment seat of Christ*" (2 Cor. 5:10, *NASB*).
5. Why do you believe God makes an eternal hell? Why do so many avoid talking about it except in profanity?
6. When you think about the wonders of heaven, what do you picture in your mind's eye?
7. How can we increase anticipation of our eternal rewards?

THIRTEEN

# PRESENT JOY

Not all the joy in life must wait until heaven. When Jesus comes into our lives He brings light and color, laughter and cheer.

Joy comes from God, and from getting outside of ourselves. Joy comes from giving, loving, lifting others.

It helps to feel the joy when we take time to give thanks—and do the simple things that produce a cheerful heart.

Oh, there will be hurts, but most of them can be good hurts. With the Holy Spirit's power and some big goals for service, we qualify for supernatural energy for the struggle.

## Monday/**Sustained**

"Joy comes not in the absence of pain but in the presence of God."[1]

Joy comes when a person gives himself away to God and to someone else.

*"Weeping may remain for a night, but rejoicing comes in the morning"* (Ps. 30:5). Joy comes when we give all our troubles to God and find His relief.

Joy comes in obeying Jesus Christ: *"I have told you this so that my joy may be in you and that your joy may be complete"* (John 15:11).

Happiness is elusive, like squeezing sand or capturing sunshine. Joy is certain, steady, always available. It's as close as Christ who dwells within you.

Joy causes you to smile through your tears, rejoice during suffering, praise God in pain. Joy comes from the Spirit, not from the body. Joy comes from God.

How do I get hold of sustained joy?

Simply by trusting God, and obeying Him one minute at a time.

Trust and praise Him in the good and happy times.

Trust and pray to Him in the hard and hurting times.

Trust and obey Him at all times.

But this alone is not enough. One more thing is needed—try giving yourself away:

> Give away a compliment, a smile, a silent prayer today.
> Give away a favor, a courtesy, a kindness. Give a helping hand to someone in need.
> Give some kind words to your family, loving words to your spouse.
> Give away your tithes and offerings to Christ through His church.
> Give away your joy, your very best, yourself.

Most of all, give yourself away to Christ in the next

minute. Right now. Ask the Holy Spirit to give you His fruit which is love, joy . . . (Gal. 5:22).

> Pray for sustained joy.
> Work at giving it to others.

## Tuesday/The White Envelope

*A woman in Baltimore, Maryland wrote the following Christmas story. Unfortunately I do not have her name. It touched my heart, and I hope it will touch yours as well.*

"It's just a small white envelope stuck among the branches of our Christmas tree; no name, no identification, no inscription. It has peeked through the branches of our Christmas tree for the past ten years or so. It all began because my husband, Mike, hated Christmas. Not the true meaning of Christmas, but the commercial aspects of it. The spending, the frantic running around at the last minute to get a tie for Uncle Harry, dusting powder for Grandma, gifts given in desperation because you couldn't think of anything else.

"Knowing he felt this way, I decided one year to bypass the usual shirts, ties, etc. and reach for something special, just for Mike. The inspiration came in an unusual way. Son Kevin, who was twelve, was wrestling at the Jr. League level and shortly before Christmas there was a non-league match between a team sponsored by an inner-city church. Mostly black, these youngsters dressed in uniforms consisting of ill-fitting boxing shorts, hole-punctured T-shirts and sneakers so ragged that the shoe strings seemed to be the only thing holding them together.

They presented a sharp contrast to our boys in their "spiffy" blue and gold uniforms and sparkling new wrestling shoes.

"As the match began, I was alarmed that the opposing team did not wear protective headgear, a luxury they obviously could not afford. Well, we ended up walloping them. We took every weight class and as each of their boys got up from the mat, he would woggle around with a kind of bravado, not willing to acknowledge defeat. "Mike said, 'I wish that just *one* of them could have won. They have a lot of potential, but losing like this could take the heart right out of them.' Mike loved kids. He knew them, having coached Little League football and baseball.

"That's when the idea for his present came. That afternoon, I went to a local sporting goods store and bought an assortment of wrestling headgear and shoes and sent them anonymously to the inner-city church. On Christmas Eve, I placed an envelope in the tree. The note inside telling Mike what I had done was his present from me. His smile was the brightest thing of Christmas that year, and for succeeding years. Each Christmas I followed the tradition; one year sending a group of retarded youngsters to a hockey game, another a check to a couple of elderly brothers whose home had burned to the ground; and on and on.

"The envelope became the highlight of our Christmas. It was always the last thing opened and our children, ignoring their new toys, would stand with wide-eyed anticipation as their Dad lifted the envelope from the tree to reveal its contents. As the children grew, the toys gave way to more practical presents, but the envelope never lost its lure.

"The story doesn't end there. You see, we lost Mike last year to dreaded cancer and when Christmas rolled around, I was still so wrapped in grief I barely got the tree up. But Christmas Eve found me placing an envelope on the tree. In the morning it was joined by three more. Each of our children had placed an envelope on the tree for their Dad. The tradition had grown and someday will expand further when our grandchildren, standing around the tree with wide-eyed anticipation, will watch as their fathers take down the envelope. Mike's spirit, like the Christmas spirit, will always be with us."

> Pray for generosity.
> Work at creativity.

## Wednesday/ Thanksgiving

Thanksgiving is the keynote of the Christian life. In the Bible it is often linked with joy and the overflowing gratitude of the heart.

For example, Paul wrote about "joyfully giving thanks" (Col. 1:11-12) and "overflowing with thankfulness" (Col. 2:7).

Funny how it works. Because of the joy of the Lord in our hearts, we give thanks to God. And as we give thanks, we feel more joy than ever.

A legend from medieval times tells of two angels sent from the throne of God to earth. One collected the petitions in people's prayers; the other gathered up thanksgivings.

The first angel returned with both arms full and a large load on his back. Everybody wanted something from God. The second scoured the earth and turned up only a handful of gratitude. Most people forgot to thank God for the wonderful things He had already given.

Thankfulness is a command in the Bible (Col. 3:15). It's a required course, not an elective in the Christian life. To live without thanksgiving is to miss the joy of worship and to dismiss the kindness of a friend.

Griping, the opposite of thanksgiving, is often a form of manipulation. It's a subtle, sometimes unconscious, attempt to get others to feel sorry for us or do something about our unhappiness.

Grateful people are happy people. Gripers make themselves miserable. Two men went fishing. One griped that he caught nothing; the other talked about the beauty of God's creation. Two women examined a bush. One complained about thorns; the other thanked God for the beauty of the flower.

Unfailing gratitude makes a human magnet out of a common personality. It's so refreshing. Thanksgiving helps us keep our sanity in the wild pace of going, doing, striving.

In fact, many of God's choice gifts are totally out of reach of our scrambling and puffing and panting to "get ahead in life."

Just think of a few:

> Salvation through our Lord Jesus Christ,
>   confidence in heaven to come,
>     satisfaction in Christ's daily presence,
>       deliverance from habits that cause misery,
>         people who love and care—family, friends,
>           church, missionaries—
>             beauty of God's created wonders,
>               truth in God's Word,
>                 power from God's Spirit,
>                   mercy from God's grace—
>                     in summary, God's lovingkindness.

No wonder the Bible exhorts us to give thanks both in spoken word and in music (Col. 3:15-16).

*"Give thanks in all circumstances, for this is God's will for you in Christ Jesus"* (1 Thess. 5:18).

```
Pray for an attitude of gratitude.
Work at continually giving thanks.
```

## Thursday/ The Secret of Cheerfulness

A stand-up comic doesn't quite do it.

> Neither does laughing it off or joking around.
> A sense of humor helps but does not guarantee the end result.

*"Even in laughter the heart may ache, and joy may end in grief"* (Prov. 14:13).

What really lifts the spirit is a cheerful heart. People with cheerful hearts
> spread joy,
> brighten up your day,
> bring encouragement,
> cause smiles,
> make you feel good.

Cheerful people are not immune from pain, trouble or tragedy.
> They face the same hard knocks of life as the rest of us.
> They simply refuse to let their spirit be crushed.

> They bounce back.
> They get up and try again.
> They laugh at themselves.
> They see the best in others.
> They find the possibilities in every problem.

*"A cheerful heart is good medicine, but a crushed spirit dries up the bones"* (Prov. 17:22).

So what is the secret of cheerfulness?

Is it personality type? In part, yes. But there is more.

Some sanguine types are all surface fluff and deftly hide their pain. Some melancholy types develop cheerful hearts that follow deep brooding. Personality alone is not the secret of a cheerful heart.

Is it positive thinking? In part, yes. But there is more.

Some people can see the possibilities in every problem, and yet they are dying on the inside. Others lack creativity and yet exude love, warmth and good cheer from the depths of their hearts. Positive thinking alone is not the secret of a cheerful heart.

Is it talent, fame, beauty, money, prestige, comfort? In part, yes. But there is more.

People who succeed with any outstanding asset or ability certainly have their moments of happiness and public recognition. If their overall lives are examined, however, long-lasting misery is often evident. Success alone is not the secret of a cheerful heart.

So what is the secret of cheerfulness? A cheerful heart comes from peace with God and love of people.

Living close to God always produces joy.

Stepping outside of ourselves to love others always generates happiness. And a life-style of joy and happiness produces a cheerful heart.

Jesus said it simply and profoundly.

> If you obey my commands, you will remain in my love, just as I have obeyed my Father's commands and remain in his love. I have told you this so that *my joy* may be in you and that *your joy* may be complete. My command is this: Love each other as I have loved you. Greater love has no one than this, that he lay down his life for his friends" (John 15:10-13, italics added).

Obey Jesus Christ.
  Love people.
    Lay down your life for your friends.
      Experience joy.
This is the secret of a cheerful heart.

---

Pray for a cheerful heart.
Work at obeying Christ and loving people.

---

## Friday/**Good Hurts**

Have you ever hurt with a good hurt?

Have you ever been so tired you could drop, and thought to yourself, "It was worth it." "I loved it." "It was worth every ounce of energy." "I'm so tired, but in my spirit I'm refreshed, challenged, stimulated."

Maybe it was after a week at summer camp. Maybe it was after teaching Sunday School. Maybe it was after cleaning up from a super church social. Maybe it was after a heavy counseling session. Maybe it was after a big workday for church. Maybe it was after a significant project on your job.

> If you have ever been given a big job by God—
> (He specializes in big jobs without pay)
> if you have been faithful to give that big job your
> best shot—
> if (especially this) you have sensed that Christ used
> you—
> ah, then you know what I am writing about.

Good hurts, but you have energy with a purpose. You have supernatural energy for the struggle.

You can understand what the apostle Paul wrote: *"I labor, struggling with all his energy, which so powerfully works in me"* (Col. 1:29).

> When you are being faithful to the Lord in your life
> and in your service—
> when you give it all you've got, calling on Christ for
> power—
> when you honestly try to keep your priorities
> straight and
> your life in balance—
> even when you fall short—
> even when you realize the task is not yet done—
> (oh, such good hurts!)
> then you experience the labor, the struggle and the
> powerful energy of Christ at work within you (see
> Col. 1:29 again).

With bad hurts, the job or marriage we hate is far from satisfying. We come home emotionally drained. We dread the next day. The psychic drainage seems almost unbearable. We feel trapped, locked-in, with no way of escape.

Buying more things, pursuing more activities, working harder on the job or the marriage—only seems to sap more energy. We feel depleted, depressed. We wonder where God is and why we feel so lousy.

Life seems to hold so little significance and we grasp for security. It reminds me of the man with a well-paying job who said to a friend of mine, "I hate what I'm doing but only seventeen more years and I retire."

How does a person move from bad hurts to good hurts, from bad tired to good tired?

Jesus Christ does not come into your life to go to sleep. Nor does He want you to lock Him in an isolated guest room of your private life. He wants to rule as Lord, blessing you with energy, stability and inner delight.

Focus your energy on developing into a major league Christian not a minor league Christian; a major league marriage not a minor league marriage; a major league servant of God not a minor league servant.

Then ask for Christ's wisdom in setting some big spiritual goals. They just might be ones you have always wanted to accomplish with Christ's power and the Spirit's gifts:

- serving someone in need—in a nursing home, a prison or simply alone and lonely,
- writing notes of encouragement,
- developing skill in witnessing,
- growing in discipleship of Christ,
- training and equipping for ministry,
- seeking the heavenly Father Himself with prayer and fasting.

Good hurts. They are worth it. A living Lord. He is

energizing. Big goals. They start us in the right direction.

Go for it!

> Pray for supernatural energy for the struggle.
> Work at setting some big goals.

## Saturday/**Morning Is Coming**

Morning is coming. I can see the redness of the early dawn on the horizon. The blackness all around is turning into silhouettes.

The beautiful color in the East is a promise. It will grow lighter and lighter. If I turn away from the light, the world is dark and despairing. The shapes of things seem haunting, foreboding. When I face the light, I'm overwhelmed with beauty. This darkness will not last forever. Morning is coming.

The color on the far horizon fades before my eyes as the light increases. The outlines and forms around me become more distinct now. It's like a world in black and white.

Nothing can stop the onward progress of morning. Almost imperceptibly, and yet I can't miss it, the light increases. Lawns and leaves turn to dark green. At least in the East, some things far away are visible.

This light will fill the sky until sunrise, until the brightness of the sun drives away the last vestige of darkness. Morning is coming. Jesus is coming.

Our Lord Jesus Christ is coming again! We look forward to His return.

Even now, by His Holy Spirit, Jesus is coming into our

lives, our churches, our families, our hearts.
His light is breaking over the horizon!

> Pray for discerning eyes.
> Work at focusing on the light.

## Sunday/ Discussion Questions

1. Name the most joyful person you know. In your opinion what sustains the joyful spirit?
2. Does your family or anyone you know have a Christmas tradition of giving to strangers? If so, explain it. Does joy result?
3. What are some practical ways to develop an attitude of gratitude? Why do we find it easier to ask God for something than to tell Christ, "thank you"?
4. Would you say that your joy is complete? (See John 15:10-13.) Why or why not?
5. In your opinion how does a person move from bad hurts to good hurts? From bad tired to good tired?
6. Share some of your big goals. Are they worthy of supernatural energy for the struggle?
7. In what ways does the light of Christ brighten our daily lives? Do you think dawn as the promise of sunrise is a fitting parable of Christ's return? Why or why not?
8. As you come to the end of this book, what have you learned about supernatural energy?

# Notes

**Chapter 1**
1. See Eph. 1:19; 3:7; 4:16; 2 Thess. 2:9 in the *New International Version*.
2. See Eph. 1:19; 3:7; 4:16; Col. 2:12 in the *New American Standard Bible*. Phil 3:21 uses "the exertion"; Col. 1:29 "power"; 2 Thess. 2:9 "the activity."
3. Does the Greek word *energeia* really mean "supernatural energy"? Yes, indeed! In G. Kittel's authoritative (and massive) *Theological Dictionary of the New Testament*, G. Bertram writes that it "is found in the sense of 'activity' or 'energy' from the pre-Socratic period." (Grand Rapids, MI: Wm. B. Eerdmans Publishing Company, 1964), 2:652. Also see word studies in major Greek commentaries.
4. Bauer, Arndt and Gingrich, *A Greek-English Lexicon of the New Testament*, (Chicago: The University of Chicago Press, 1957), p. 264. Also see H. C. Hahn, "Work, Do, Accomplish" in Colin Brown, ed., *The New International Dictionary of New Testament Theology* (Grand Rapids, MI: Zondervan Publishing House, 1978), 3:1147, 1151-52.
5. Some translations of the New Testament *do* communicate the essential meaning of "supernatural energy" in current English synonyms. See *Jerusalem Bible, New English Bible, Today's English Version* and *Phillips* as examples.
6. In the *New American Standard Bible* see Matt. 14:12; Mark 6:14; Rom. 7:5; 1 Cor. 12:6,11;, 2 Cor. 1:6; 4:12; Gal. 2:8; 3:5; 5:6; Eph. 1:11,20; 2:2; 3:20; Phil. 2:13; Col. 1:29; 1 Thess. 2:13; 2 Thess. 2:7.

**Chapter 2**
1. Dr. Larry Crabb, *Inside Out* (Colorado Springs: Navpress, 1988), pp. 116-129.
2. Peter Drucker's address was given at the Effective Management Ministry and Leadership Conference at the Pasadena Convention Center on April 27, 1988. The Conference was sponsored by the Institute for Organizational Development of Fuller Theological Seminary.


**Chapter 3**
1. Covert Bailey, *Fit or Fat?* (Boston: Houghton Mifflin Company, 1977, 1978), pp. 23-28.
2. Archibald D. Hart, *Adrenalin and Stress* (Waco, TX: Word Books, 1986, 1988), pp. 149-164.
3. George Eldon Ladd, *New Testament Theology* (Grand Rapids, MI: William B. Eerdmans Publishing Company, 1974), p. 370.


**Chapter 4**
1. Quoted by Mrs. Charles E. Cowman, *Streams in the Desert*, vol. 1 (Grand Rapids, MI: Zondervan Publishing House, 1965), p. 274.
2. Eleanor L. Doan, ed., *Speakers Sourcebook* (Grand Rapids, MI: Zondervan Publishing House), 1960, p. 203.


**Chapter 5**
1. A term for spiritual warfare used by George Fox and other early Friends in the 17th century.
2. David Bryant, *Concerts of Prayer* (Ventura, CA: Regal Books, 1984), p. 197.
3. S.D. Gordon, *Quiet Talks on Prayer* (Old Tappan, NJ: Fleming H. Revell Co., n.d.), p. 16.
4. Howard R. Macy, *Rhythms of the Inner Life*, (Old Tappan, NJ:Fleming H. Revell Co., 1988), p. 25.
5. Charles Mylander, *Running the Red Lights: Putting the Brakes on Sexual Temptation*, (Ventura, CA: Regal Books, 1986), pp. 86-90.


**Chapter 7**
1. D. Elton Trueblood, *The Predicament of Modern Man* (New York: Harper & Row, Publishers, 1944), pp. 56,60.
2. Charles Colson, "A New Barbarian Invasion," *Jubilee: The Monthly Newsletter of Prison Fellowship*, July 1988, p. 7.
3. Rich Buhler, *Love, No Strings Attached* (Nashville: Thomas Nelson Publishers, 1987), pp. 18,27-28,50.
4. Ibid., pp. 101-121.

## Chapter 8

1. This is adopted from a story by Bob Benson which reminded me of this experience in my own life. See R. Benson, ed., *See You at the House: The Stories Bob Benson Used to Tell,* (Nashville, TN: Generoux, 1986), pp. 68-69.
2. "The Love of God" by F. M. Lehman. © 1917. Renewed 1945, by Nazarene Publishing House. All rights reserved. Used by permission.

## Chapter 9

1. Dr. Larry Crabb, *Inside Out* (Colorado Springs: Navpress, 1988), p. 83.

## Chapter 10

1. Jess Moody in Lloyd Cary, comp., *Quotable Quotations* (Wheaton, IL: Victor Books, 1985), p. 76.
2. Sherri McAdam, quoted in Richard J. Foster, *Money, Sex and Power* (San Francisco: Harper & Row, Publishers), p. 196.
3. Clyde Murdock, *A Treasury of Humor* (Grand Rapids, MI: Zondervan Publishing House, 1967), p. 62.
4. Frank S. Mead, ed., *The Encyclopedia of Religious Quotations* (Old Tappan, NJ: Fleming H. Revell, 1965), p. 238.

## Chapter 11

1. Mark Twain, quoted in Bob Phillips, *A Time to Laugh* (Eugene, OR: Harvest House Publishers), p. 76.
2. Charles Reade, quoted in Phillips, *A Time to Laugh.*
3. I am indebted to Dr. Larry Crabb for his writing on the concepts of unmet longings, self-protective behaviors and "demandingness." I highly recommend his book, *Inside Out* (Colorado Springs: Navpress, 1988).

## Chapter 12

1. I am indebted to the New Testament scholar George Eldon Ladd for enlightening these biblical concepts. His scholarly book, *The Presence of the Future,* gives a full presentation. Easier to understand is his textbook, *A Theology of the New Testament* (Grand Rapids, MI: William B. Eerdmans Publishing Company, 1974), pp. 68-69.
2. Julia Ward Howe, "Battle Hymn of the Republic," 1861, stanza 1. Public domain.
3. Helmut Thielicke, *The Silence of God,* trans., G.W. Bromiley (Grand Rapids MI: William B. Eerdmans Publishing Co., 1962), pp. 77-88.
4. William Barclay, *The Daily Study Bible Series,* rev. ed. *The Revelation of John,* vol. 2 (Philadelphia: The Westminster Press, 1976), p. 252.
5. Billy Graham, *Approaching Hoofbeats, The Four Horsemen of the Apocalypse,* (Minneapolis, MN: Grason, 1983), p. 203.

## Chapter 13

1. Author unknown.

# More Regal books to help you tap into His supernatural energy!

**When the Pressure's On—Gene Getz**   Gain a greater understanding of God's faithful intervention when the pressure's on in this study of Elijah.  See how God can multiply your effectiveness as you recognize His continual presence and power in your life.   ISBN 0-8307-0923-1 5418100

**You Can Pray with Power—Lloyd John Ogilvie** Discover what God meant prayer to be and what He has said about the secret dynamic conversation with Him when we pray.   ISBN 0-8307-1248-8   5419257

**Today Can Be Different—Harold Sala**   A short compilation of 365 guidelines for daily living that are positive and uplifting.  These readings are certain to strengthen your faith in God.
ISBN 0-8307-1322-0   5419690

**God's Transforming Love—Lloyd John Ogilvie**   Daily reflections on God's life-changing power from Lloyd John Ogilvie's classics are brought together in this enduring collection of devotions.  ISBN 0-8307-1320-4   5111794

### Find these and other Regal books at your local Christian retailer.